THE OAK ISLAND CODE
Deciphering the origins and movements of the treasure with data science

DAVID JAMES IVELL

Copyright © 2023 David James Ivell

Pocket Book Company

All rights reserved.

ISBN: 978-1-916989-01-6

CONTENTS

	Foreword	page
1	Oak Island	3
2	Origins of the treasure	15
3	The Siege of Havana	29
4	William Nurenburg & Oak Island	35
5	The Sinking of the London	39
6	The Manso Tontine	53
7	The Tontine of 1882	59
8	The Chambercombe Manor Connection	63
9	The Portland Oregon Connection	69
10	The Florida Connection	73
11	Mary Buckingham	79
12	So where else could the treasure be?	81
13	The Pirates Graveyard	87
14	Gracia Real de Santa Teresa de Mose	91
15	Forensic Science and Lidar Mapping	97
16	What happened to Captain William Robinson (Robertson)?	103
17	The other Manso Lineage	111
18	Timeline	113
19	Barings Bank	119
20	Familia Manso	121
21	The Oak Island Code - Conclusion	125
	About the Author	

FOREWORD

Who, as a child, didn't imagine finding a treasure map?

Today's children may dream of being zombie hunters or social media stars, but I wanted to be a pirate, with a curved cutlass and a Jolly Roger on my bedroom wall, drawing treasure maps rather than doing my homework. I blame my dad of course, whose favourite book was Treasure Island by Robert Louis Stevenson, and it was that book that sent me to sleep dreaming.

My career unfortunately hasn't provided too many opportunities for piracy, but it has enabled me to take another adventure into data science. Not the same, you say? But for centuries, maps have often been told rather than drawn, communicated through stories that we can remember. Stories told around a campfire by a visiting stranger, or passed down through generations within the same family, or even in the folklore of a culture. One thing is for sure: we all like a good treasure story.

Rather than a church spire, a gnarled tree on a hill, a sea monster, or an X marking the spot, a landmark on a treasure map may equally be an event in time, an article in a newspaper, a record in an archive, or a painting painted centuries after the event.

In the past few years, there has been a revolution in how we think about treasure hunting. Instead of digging through soil like archaeologists looking for ancient artifacts, the future involves digging through data. There is a lot of data, covering every imaginable facet of our lives and the lives of our predecessors. More and more records that previously sat on dusty shelves are now being digitized and made available online. Investigations that in the past would have required researchers to wade through records in libraries all over the world can now be conducted from their laptops in seconds.

I am a modern day treasure hunter! I have ditched the pith helmet and spade and have a whole suite of algorithms in my kit bag. Please join me on an adventure.

CHAPTER 1

OAK ISLAND

There are a lot of theories and stories surrounding hidden treasure buried on Oak Island, Nova Scotia, in something called the Money-Pit. There are books and TV series and there have been numerous attempts over the years to try and tunnel down to find it. However, the treasure has never been found, and why? Because it's not where people think it is!

As any successful treasure hunter will tell you, to find treasure, you first need to have a good idea of what treasure you are looking for. This may seem obvious, but it is amazing how many treasure hunters have failed to do even the most basic research into the treasure they are seeking. The "stumble across it" method has been lucky for some but, for most of us, relying on luck will have no better odds than winning the lottery.

To put it simply, if you know what you are looking for, you have a better chance of understanding how and where to find it. You will also be better equipped to avoid destroying the treasure, or pushing it further out of reach in the process of recovering it.

While not all treasures are protected by booby traps, like those seen in the Indiana Jones films, many are. Treasures that are hidden in tombs or other concealed locations may be protected by traps such as decoy chambers, mud pits, false floors, and spear pits. They may also be flooded or buried underground, something that has clearly frustrated the treasure hunters at Oak Island. The mistakes made during the historic botched attempts to retrieve the treasure that was presumed to be on Oak Island made it almost impossible for future treasure hunters to investigate.

Those early treasure hunters are a prime example of what happens when you start a hunt without knowing what you are looking for and without understanding the best way to retrieve it. They have spent years digging on the island, but they have yet to find the treasure they are seeking. This is because they did not do their research and they did not understand the challenges they would face.

If you are serious about finding treasure, it is important to do your due diligence and understand the challenges ahead. You should also be prepared to invest time and money in the research. The more research you do, the less money you will spend. With careful planning and execution, you may just be the next person to find a hidden treasure.

Treasure hunting 101: The most important and basic concept is to figure out where the treasure came from, what form the treasure may take, and if there are any trails of it being moved elsewhere before you even start. This will help determine where the treasure is actually located and will save a lot of time looking in the wrong place. Treasure is rarely hidden by mistake. The person who hid the treasure knew exactly where they put it and how to retrieve it. You need to understand that person and what pressures the person who hid the treasure may have been under at that time. Also what skills had their career equipped them with which they may have used to plan to keep their fortune safe? Was it hidden for safekeeping, or was it intended to be used for a specific purpose? Was it hidden in a hurry or was it a well planned and executed event?

At the very minimum you should know what the historical context was in which the treasure was hidden? Was it hidden during a war, a natural disaster, or a financial crisis? What was the purpose of the treasure? Why was it hidden? What was the value of the treasure? Was it made of gold, silver, jewels, paper, or other valuable materials? What was the size and weight of the treasure? All these things will point to where practically it might be.

Once you have a good understanding of what form the treasure may take, you can start to follow the trail to where it is located. Are there any historical records that mention the treasure or the world events that surrounded the time of it being hidden? These records could provide you with valuable information about the treasure's location, such as the name of the person who hid it, the year it was hidden, or the likely locations where it might be found. If you were very lucky there could be a map, but that is most unlikely because very few treasures have actually been found by referring to a treasure map. Why? Because the person who is trying to protect the treasure wouldn't risk writing it down.

Are there any stories or legends about the treasure? These stories could provide you with hugely valuable additional information about its location or its history.

If you are able to find enough clues, you should be able to start to follow the trail to the treasure. However, it is important to remember that treasure hunting is a challenging and time-consuming endeavour. It is important to be patient and persistent if you want to be successful.

One hypothesis I have read was that the treasure at Oak Island was buried by the Knights Templar in the 14th century. The Templars were a wealthy and powerful military order of skilled engineers and builders with the potential to construct the complex system of tunnels and traps that have been found on the island. The Knights Templar were disbanded on Friday, October 13, 1312, by Pope Clement V, which to this day is why we see Friday the 13th as unlucky! The order had been accused of heresy and other crimes, and the Pope and King of France, who owed the Knights Templar a lot of money, ordered that all of their property be seized and that the last Grand Master of the Knights Templar, Jacques de Molay, was to be burned at the stake. Friday the 13th was certainly unlucky for him!

The disbandment of the Knights Templar was a major event in European history. The order had been a powerful military force for centuries, and its dissolution left a power vacuum that was filled by other groups, such as the Hospitallers and the Teutonic Knights.

The disbandment of the Knights Templar is also associated with many superstitions and conspiracy theories. Some people believe that the order was not disbanded at all, but that it went underground and continues to exist to this day. Others believe that the vast treasure of the Knights Templar is hidden somewhere, and that it is waiting to be found by someone who is worthy.

Another theory about the Oak Island treasure is that it was buried by Captain William Kidd, a Scottish pirate who was active in the early 18th century. Kidd is known to have buried treasure on several islands in the Caribbean, including Gardiner's Island, Long Island, and Rum Cay. Some believed it is possible that he also buried treasure on Oak Island. Kidd was executed for piracy on 23 May 1701 at Execution Dock in Wapping in London.

There are many more theories found on the internet ranging from the French fortune of Mary Antoinette, Shakespear's manuscripts, French valuables from Louisbourg, Vikings, even the Holy Grail!

Whatever the theory it is clear there was indeed treasure once there on Oak Island. In 1796, it is well documented that a group of young boys from afar observed some strange lights on the island one night and the next day went to investigate. What they found was the marks of an excavation having taken place of a deep hole on the Island. The hole was about 100 feet deep and lined with wooden planks and coconut husks. The boys dug down into the hole, but they soon encountered a layer of seawater as the tunnel began to fill that prevented them from going any further. The assumption the boys made, as have future generations of treasure hunters and TV producers, was that the lights the boys had seen pointed to treasure being buried on the island.

Over the years, many people have attempted to find the treasure at Oak Island. However, no one has been successful.

The treasure has been called "the most expensive treasure hunt in history", and it is estimated that over $100 million has been spent on the search.

To the annoyance, I am sure, of everyone currently digging there however is that, if they had done their due diligence and historical research, it would have been clear that what the boys had seen from afar on that night in 1796 was not treasure being buried at all, the treasure was actually being skillfully removed before being transported to England.

A few trinkets may have been lost whilst the treasure was being recovered from the Money-Pit and the fortune may be long gone from Oak Island, but one thing is for sure, it is still out there to be found! Everyone is just looking in the wrong place! That fortune has a present day value of over $18 billion dollars. It has been hunted by many and every day it is a step closer to being found as new data sets appear. If you can link the clues, it might even be you who finds it!

In the past few years, there has been a revolution in how we think about treasure hunting. Instead of digging through soil like archaeologists looking for ancient artifacts, the future involves digging through data. There is a lot of data, covering every imaginable facet of our lives and the lives of our predecessors. More and more records that previously sat on dusty shelves are now being digitized and made available online. Investigations that in the past would have required researchers to wade through records in libraries all over the world can now be conducted from their laptops in seconds.

We would all like to find a treasure map, wouldn't we? But a map doesn't have to be a piece of paper. Throughout the centuries, maps have often been told rather than drawn, and communicated through stories that we can remember.

Stories told around a campfire by a visiting stranger, or passed down through generations within the same family, or even in the folklore of a culture. One thing is for sure, we all like a good treasure story.

Rather than a church spire, a gnarled tree on a hill, a sea monster, or an X marking the spot, a landmark on a treasure map may equally be an event in time, an article in a newspaper, a record in an archive, or a painting, painted centuries after the event.

Paper maps only record a moment in time, but following a trail through data can record directions across centuries.

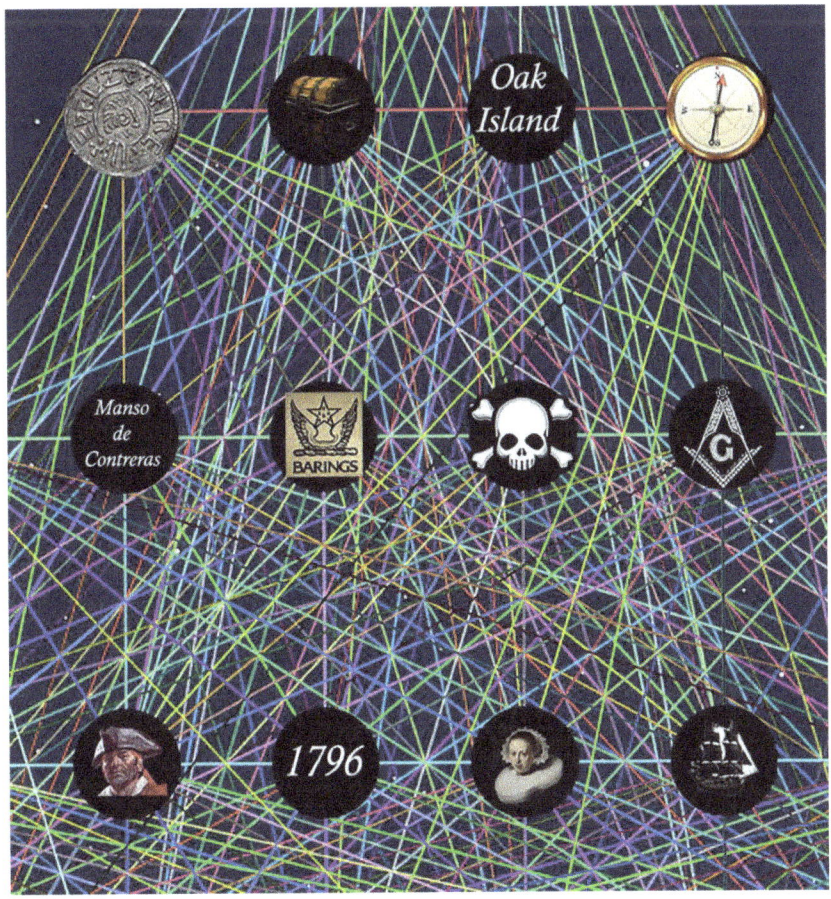

The power of data science is not always easy to understand, so let's make an analogy. Imagine the United Kingdom national football stadium in London, called Wembley. When it is full, it has 90,000 people watching the game. Suppose each of those people had a unique pile of books, old newspapers, shipping records, names, dates and bank records, a pile as tall as their head in front of them. Now imagine they are all tasked with reading through all that information looking for that one clue, a needle-in-a-haystack, that relates to the locations, people, and movement of ships and money, hundreds of years ago, or even an event that happened today. Then when they find something that might be interesting, but they are not quite sure if it may be important or not, they must speak to all the other 90,000 people to see if they too have come across that same name or date in their pile of papers. If, after shouting out to everyone in the stadium, they found someone who had spotted something similar and that name was written in conjunction with a second name, perhaps a ship or a date, then the same person would have to speak to everyone again about this new piece of information. We would have 90,000 people reading a little but then trying to talk, again and again, to everyone else about their own pieces of information. Chaos!

This is how research used to be done, mostly by letters or emails sent between people or institutions such as museum with information archives. It was slow, took a lot of resources, and was not accurate. The equivalent using data science will enable us to capture all that information and complete the same search across all that data in under 5 minutes. We can spot patterns that we just wouldn't be able to see with the naked eye. When a new database of records comes online, we add it to the search, and within seconds we can see where patterns emerge. From those patterns, we can identify the leads we want to follow. It's a sign of the times, but now the accuracy of a computer comparing documents is more accurate than a human.

Imagine a computer, reading two sentences. How old are you? and, what is your age? They are two sentences constructed very differently but actually mean the same thing. Until recently it would have been almost impossible for a computer to understand that they meant the same, but now they can, and they do it very, very well! Now we can not only process huge volumes of data, but we can also understand the sentiment of what is being said, and most importantly, spot patterns, links and relationships.

Following a trail of events and actions across time can be challenging for a number of reasons.

First, the sheer volume of data that needs to be analysed can be overwhelming. There are billions of documents, images, and other records that have been created over the course of human history. This data is then stored in a variety of formats, making it difficult to search and analyse.

Second, the languages that are used to describe events can vary widely. For example, a historical event might be described in English, French, Spanish, or any number of other languages. This can make it difficult to identify and connect related events.

Finally, even if the same event is described in the same language, it may be described differently by different people. This is because people may have different perspectives on the event, or they may be trying to convey different information.

Despite these challenges, data science is making it possible to follow trails of events and actions across time in ways that were never before possible. This information can be used to reconstruct past events, understand historical trends, and make predictions about the future.

The world around us is becoming increasingly interconnected as communication technologies proliferate and the cost of digital data storage plummets. Meanwhile, scientific equipment is being pointed both into space and into the depths of our past. The explosion in science is matched by advances in computing, which are now sophisticated enough to handle immense amounts of data.

This is the emergence of the new field of big data, data science and AI (Artificial Intelligence). Data scientists are the postmodern treasure hunters. They will reach into their toolboxes of algorithms and dig into data looking for hidden correlations, trying to find never-before-seen patterns with the hope of advancing the frontier of knowledge and supporting the development of new knowledge.

The effort and meticulousness involved are reminiscent of criminal detective work and everyday millions of new data records are generated, stored and processed.

The relationships in the data create various different hypotheses, that are then investigated to see what evidence exists to prove or dis-prove their authenticity and fill the gaps in the story. It is like a novel, where the different chapters are written but distributed in different locations. The clues in the data are enabling us to find them, one by one!

The trail to this lost fortune had been cold for many years, but now data scientists are able to pull together massive data sets of ship movements, articles written in historical newspapers and journals, and look for patterns in the data that previously would be impossible to spot by the human eye. Patterns of linked dates, people, relationships and movement of goods and money. With links to the British Siege of Havana, the mysterious activities on Oak Island, and the scuttling of a British ship, "The London", with chests of treasure, French prisoners of war and slaves, in the Devon town of Ilfracombe. We are back on the trail!

THE OAK ISLAND CODE

CHAPTER 2

ORIGINS OF THE TREASURE

Where does the data tell us the treasure came from and how did it get to Oak Island?

From Spain to Havanna

In 1597, Francisco Manso de Contreras, a gentleman (Hidalgo), was approached by his cousin, the Duke of Lerma, who was acting as Regent for The King of Spain, Felipe III, or de facto prime minister, to take up an assignment as Chief Justice for the King's Spanish colonies in the Caribbean. Lerma, known as the King's Favourite or sometimes unfavourably as the King's Shadow, was known for his Machiavellian manipulation of the Royal courts of Europe to enhance his influence.

One of the most popular plays of the period at the Theatre Royal, Drury Lane in London was The Great Favourite by Sir Robert Howard, depicting Lerma as an unscrupulous, cynical, and blasphemous manipulator. It was premiered to the English King Charles II and even starred the famous mistress of the King, Nell Gwyn, who played Lerma's daughter.

Lerma's appointment of Francisco as Chief Justice was very likely to have been a political appointment to either assist his influence or increase his wealth. There is also a possibility he intended to remove Francisco from "accompanying" Margaret of Austria who was betrothed to the King and who had become close friends with Francisco in the years preceding her marriage in 1599. Margaret's PR was of a lady of discretion and virtue, which would be perfect for the wife of a King, and this marriage between the most important families in the world could not be rocked by scandal. Whether flirtatious or not, a close friendship between them might not have been welcome. Both Francisco and Margaret were in the Italian town of Ferrara in the years preceeding her marriage.

Francisco and the Duke of Lerma had also both been politically close to the previous Queen of Felipe II, Mary I of England, and they reputedly held lands in England in the region of the Isle of Portland. There were certainly close contacts between the Manso family and English senior members of court that continued for the next two centuries. It was also rumoured that Francisco's mother Beatriz Zapata de Contreras was an illegitimate child of King Carlos I of Spain, being conceived before the marriage with Isabella of Portugal, and although not recognised, had her own connections at court.

As well as implementing Spanish law, Francisco was also tasked with eliminating the threat from piracy, which was reducing the Spanish treasury. Although deterrence was the key aim, as was usual Francisco was rewarded by being allowed to take a small percentage of any confiscated gold, jewels or slaves as his compensation.

With a fine deep-water harbour, reached from the sea by a mile-long channel, containing the largest Spanish ship yard, Havana was the most important port in the Spanish American colonies commercially and politically. It was the base for a strong navel squadron and the rendezvous for the treasure ships sailing between the Spanish South American colonies and Spain, The Flota. Cuba's strategic importance to Spain and the heart of the Spanish finances in the Caribbean made it an obvious location for Francisco to be based.

In 1603 he moved to Cuba, settling in Remedios with his wife Eugenia Simon y Pica, from Becerril de Campos, 14 years his senior. They didn't have any children. In 1606 Francisco invited his younger brother Antonio Manso de Contreras, his wife, Maria Catalina Rodriguez de Mendoza, and family to join him in Remedios. Before Antonio sailed from Spain, he got the King's blessing and increased powers to accelerate seizing valuables from non-Spanish ships granted to him by the Duke of Lerma.

Andreas Contreras

Antonio and Francisco more than doubled their wealth over the next 5 years and assuredly made the Duke of Lerma, even more wealthy with regular donations to him personally as well as the revenues to the King. Antonio had 3 sons, Nicolas, Tomas and Captain Andres Manso de Contreras, but it was only Andres who had children of his own with his wife, Antonia Armonia del Campo y Rodriguez de Arciniega. They had many children with their sons being Nicolas, Luciano, Tomas and Bartolome (b.1680). Bartolome was the natural successor and cleverly grew the family fortune, including expanding it with new lands in Florida. The largest portion of the Manso fortune that was held in money chests (opposed to property or slaves) was moved to Yaguajay when Bartolome purchased, for $4,500, the hacienda in July 1697 from Gonzales de la Cruz y Crespo (Jose), a priest who was a close family friend and who had baptised Isabel Hernandez de Medina y Vida in 1671. There was also a strong room reputedly buried partly underwater on the small island of Cayo Santa Maria.

Bartolome married Isabel Hernandez de Medina y Vidal who then passed his inheritance to his son also named Bartolome. When Bartolome the younger married Josefina de Loyola y Monteagudo, they had four children. The heir, Luis, who under Spanish Law should have inherited - died in infancy, and the three girls, María Isabel del Santísimo Sacramento, María Dolores de la Resurrección and María Manuela de San Agustín, ended up as cloistered nuns in the convent of Santa Clara in the City of Havana where their family friend and priest Gonzales de La Cruz y Crespo was buried.

Bartolome's wealth continued to grow from his properties as well as his navel exploits. He was the owner of land spreading through Cuba; Seibabo, Santa Cruz, Guainbo, Yaguajay, Centeno, San Augustin, Mayajigua, Hato de Caguanes and up to the Jatibonico del Norte river and the old province of Villarena up to Sancti Spiritus.

With threats of revolutions in America and France, the Spanish Empire and the "old world" was seen to be in decline. Spain was heavily in debt and was searching for fortunes wherever it could find them. Political corruption was sowing seeds of discontent, and the ideologies of "liberty, equality, and democracy" were circulating. These ideas were starting to challenge not only the traditional order but even the traditional authority of the church. Increasingly worried about world events, Bartolome ordered his daughters to hide a small part of the fortune for safety at the convent as a precaution, speculated to be six iron chests loaded with massive gold ingots and family jewels. The newspaper El País describes in detail the exact site of the embedment: the wall over the monumental arch of the door of the convent of Santa Clara in the City of Havana.

ANCIENT CONVENT OF SANTA CLARA, HAVANA, CUBA.

By 1704, they decided at least some of their wealth should be moved to a bank overseas for safety. At this time the London and Amsterdam banks had started issuing promissory notes, enabling wealth to be more easily transferable. Large amounts of gold, silver, and jewellery from the Manso fortune, were sent in-secret to Europe. The new banks enabled wealth to be loaned to many people and not held in one place where it could be seized. Simply the risk was spread over hundreds of people. The data science suggests a number of banks are named as the potential beneficiary of this particular deposit; Bank Odd Fellow, Conrad Bank, The Bank of England, and various Goldsmiths of the time, however there is more evidence that the value of the deposit was either entered into a financial instrument of the time called a Tontine or another financial instrument managed by Sir William Paterson.

A [tontine](#) is a form of life annuity with, in the terminology of the eighteenth century, the benefit of survivorship. The tontine concept was named after a Neapolitan Lorenzo Tonti, who first proposed his financing scheme in 1652. There were four roles within a tontine. The issuer was the borrower and initiator of the tontine. The subscriber provided the initial capital subscription and when doing so had to nominate a life. The shareholder or proprietor was the person or cartel entitled to receive the annual interest on the tontine share, a payment often referred to as the dividend. The nominee was the person on whose life the contract was contingent. The total annual dividend paid by the issuer remained unchanged but as nominees died, shareholders whose nominees were still living received an increased dividend as the total was divided between fewer people. Eventually the shareholder whose nominee was the one remaining survivor received the whole dividend. The issuer did not have to repay the capital sum but had a commitment to pay the dividend for as long as there were any survivors. The beneficiaries, cousins of the three nuns had payments made in London, Oxford or Amsterdam.

Sir William Paterson lived from April 1658 to 22 January 1719. He was the founder of the Bank of England and influential in starting the Bank of Scotland; he was also the architect of the disastrous Darien Scheme and one of the negotiators behind the Acts of Union bringing together Scotland and England in 1707. At the age of 17 he went to Bristol, and from there to the Bahamas. Here he became a prosperous merchant by a variety of means, including, some have suggested, activities that bordered on piracy. It is here that Paterson became acquainted with Bartolome Manso de Contreras. That he knew and obtained information from

Pirate Captains Sharpe, Dampier, Wafer, and Sir Henry Morgan (the taker of Panama), is indeed referenced in the data. From the Bahamas he moved to Holland, where he invested his fortune in Dutch Banks. He also returned from the Caribbean with a strong belief that the establishment of a trading company in Panama would open up huge potential, allowing trading to take place across the Atlantic and the Pacific (in effect pre-empting the reasons for the construction of the Panama Canal over two centuries later). The complication with such an idea was that it would inevitably be opposed by the Spanish, who already had strong interests in Central America. Paterson returned to London from Holland and published a document called "A Brief Account of the Intended Bank of England" under which a central bank would be set up to help with Government finance. The English King Willian II approved of the idea and in July 1694 the Bank was established by Royal Charter and made its first loan to the Government of £1.2m. Paterson became one of the Directors of the Bank of England, a post he was removed from as soon as the following year after a financial scandal. He raised money for his controversial scheme to build a new colony at the Gulf of Darian, Panama, called New Caledonia, that turned disastrous for all those involved. Among 80% of participants died within the first year, mostly through disease, including his second wife and child. It was then abandoned in March 1700 after a siege by Spanish forces, which blockaded the harbour. Paterson's investors included many private rich overseas investors, and as the Company of Scotland, was backed by approximately 20% of all the money circulating in Scotland, its failure left the entire Scottish Lowlands in financial ruin. On Sir William Paterson's return to Scotland he had been virtually bankrupted by Darien, so he resumed his trading, backed by wealthy private clients, including the Manso family, which was accounted for at the Bank of England under the name of William Paterson.

However, The Manso family had not placed all trust in the new banking system and it was decided that a part of the fortune would be transported to Santa Rosa de la Eminencia, Margarita, where family descending from another branch of the Manso family now lived. Francisca had emigrated to Isle Magarita in 1585 and several other members of the Manso lineage had held positions of authority there, including Margarita's representation in Spain. There is a less reliable report in newspapers of the time that a heavy transport of 7 chests from the Manso family were taken to a convent in Puerto Rico in 1710, either Convento de Porta Coeli, or, Basilica Menor de San Juan Bautista y Parroquia Nuestra Señora de los Remedios.

It is known that large bank deposits were made at periods of uncertainty, such as the American War-of-Independence in 1776, and The French Revolution in 1789. But there was also a transfer in 1762, after the fall of Havana to the British.

There are records that in 1776, at the time of the American

War of Independence, that a shipment was made - a combination of four chests delivered to the dock from "The Hacienda" at Yaguajay, and three chests stored at the Convent. These chests were placed aboard a sailing ship flying Dutch colours, El Titán under Master Tomas Morrison, accompanied by Jose Manso de Contreras y Perez del Prado, on route for England and an English Bank or Goldsmith.

Earlier, when Spain joined France in the Seven Years War against the British, the British reacted quickly, and sent a huge expedition under the leadership of Lord Albemarle. He laid siege and captured the city of Havana in Cuba. Havana, located over the Gulf Stream, was the fastest route for ships sailing from America to Europe, was more populated than either Boston or New York, held the heart of the Spanish fleet in the Caribbean, and was key to Spain's influence in the region.

The speed of the British armada's assembly consisting of nearly 13,000 soldiers, 17,000 sailors and marines, 23 ships of the line, 19 auxiliary warships, and 160 transports was key, as when they arrived at Havana, the Spanish were completely unprepared and succumbed.

> AMERICA.
> Charles Town, South Carolina, Aug. 18. On Saturday last arrived here, in seven weeks from England, his Majesty's ship Success, Capt. Botterell, sent here as a stationed ship for the protection of this province, in consequence of an application made by his Excellency our Governor.
>
> *New York, Sept. 6. Last night arrived 15 transports from the Havana. There were 30 sail of transports left the Havana for this port; having the 17th regiment, the two batalions of Royal Highlanders, and Montgomerie's on board, mostly sick; but only fifteen arrived here with their convoy, the Enterprise of 40 guns, and Porcupine men of war, having parted with the others two days after they left the Havana; who, it was imagined, joined the fleet from Jamaica of a hundred sail then beating through for Europe.*
>
> *New York, Sept 6. Last night arrived 15 transports from Havana. There were 30 sail of transports left the Havana for this port; saving the 17th regiment, the two batalions of the Royal Highlanders, and Montgomories on board.* 𝕿𝖍𝖊 𝕷𝖔𝖓𝖉𝖔𝖓 𝕮𝖍𝖗𝖔𝖓𝖎𝖈𝖑𝖊:

On the evening of the sixth of September, 1762, a convoy of 30 transports from Havana arrived in New York. Four transport ships, carrying British troops from the Royal Highlanders Regiment, continued onwards on their journey documented in their logbook for London, via Halifax, they were commissioned to transport a deposit from the Manso family.

According to the logbooks the weather had turned and the seas were stormy. The Transports travelled closer to the East coast and up towards Nova Scotia.

For reasons unknown, at least as yet, as they reached Nova Scotia, the four transport ships split, with two taking refuge at Bridgewater, whilst the other two continued their journey towards London, escorted by His Majesty's Ship, Aldborough, who had left Quebec on the 10th of September. They arrived in Plymouth, as opposed to London, on the thirtieth of October. The chests were unloaded and signed-for by Francis Baring, a son of an Exeter Wool Trader.

In 1762, a new bank, becoming the UK's oldest merchant bank, was founded by Francis and John Baring. Another backer of this new bank was Luis Manso de Contreras, a member of the Manso family, who had been educated in Winchester College and Cambridge University and served as ambassador to Russia from 1777 to 1780. This may have been the start of Barings profitable relationship in Russia. By 1890 The Manso family was one of the banks largest shareholders.

Barings Bank went on to finance the United States government's purchase of Louisiana from Napoleon Bonaparte in 1803. This doubled the size of The United States. After a $3 million down payment in gold, the remainder of the purchase was made in United States bonds, which Napoleon sold to Barings through Hope & Co. of Amsterdam.

Barings had an illustrious client list, including The Russian Royal Family, Bonaparte's nephew, Napoleon III, and later US Presidents, James Monroe and Franklin Roosevelt. By 1818, Barings was called, "the sixth great European power", after England, France, Prussia, Austria and Russia.

THE OAK ISLAND CODE

CHAPTER 3

THE SIEGE OF HAVANA

In June 1762, a British force consisting of nearly 13,000 soldiers, 17,000 sailors and marines, 23 ships of the line, 19 auxiliary warships, and 160 transports, making it possibly the largest military expedition ever seen in the America's, arrived in Havana in the midst of the Seven Years' War. By mid-August 1762, the British expedition had conquered the city. The jubilation of Britons and British Americans was immediate and the cost of losing Havana to Spain, the most important city in the Americas, more influential than Boston and New York combined, was immense. Although Britain only retained Havana for 11 months, she had captured a large proportion of the Spanish fleet, disabled Spanish trade, sent Spain's finances into freefall with the disruption to the Flota, the annual transport of gold and silver from America to Spain, and seized the Spanish gold reserves. It wasn't until Spain ceded Florida that the British handed Havana back. In these 11 months the Manso family continued to prosper under British occupation as they already had good links with British nobility and business. It was clear that Britain had become the new superpower in the region and the future of Cuba would likely be comparable to the other Caribbean islands which could often change hands. This could put their fortune at risk.

HM warships: Namur 90 guns (flag ship), Valiant 74 guns, Cambridge 80 guns, Culloden 74 guns, Temeraire 74 guns, Dublin 74 guns, Dragon 74 guns, Temple 70 guns, Marlborough 68 guns, Orford 66 guns, Belleisle 64 guns, Hampton Court 64 guns, Stirling Castle 64 guns, Devonshire 66 guns, Pembroke 60 guns, Ripon 60 guns, Nottingham 60 guns, Edgar 60 guns, Defiance 60 guns, Sutherland 50 guns, Dover 44 guns, Alarm 38 guns, Echo 22 guns, Mercury 22 guns, Cygnet 18 guns, Thunder 10 guns, Grenado, Bonetta, Basilisk bomb ships, Lurcher cutter.

HMS Hussar was lost off Cape Francois before Pocock's Fleet began the voyage up the Old Bahamas Channel.

In addition, there were some 150 merchant ships carrying troops, equipment and supplies. This included The London and The New Adventure who are very important in our story as you will soon discover.

In a return dated 23rd May 1762 the regiments were listed as 'Under the command of Lieutenant General Lord Albemarle': 1st, 4th, 9th, 15th, 17th, 22nd, 27th, 28th, 32nd, 35th, 40th,

1st and 2nd Battalions of 42nd, 43rd, 48th, 56th, 3rd/60th, 65th, 72nd, 77th, 90th, 95th Regiments (the 34th and 66th are not included in this return at this point but were mentioned in dispatches of injured or sick troops).

The total of troops given in the return was 11,998 (perhaps 12,500 with the 34th), of whom 1,289 were sick.

It was also reported that some 500 Royal Artillery personnel were present with Albemarle's army.

At the end of July 1762, the 46th and 58th Regiments, Gorham's Rangers and other provincial troops commanded by Colonel Burton joined Albemarle's army.

The Seven Years War broke out in 1756, with most notably the French loss of Canada to Great Britain. In 1761 King Carlos III of Spain signed a secret treaty of mutual defensive and offensive support with his fellow Bourbon, King Louis XVI of France. However, this secret treaty was discovered in 1762 by spies working for Sir John Montague, 4th Earl of Sandwich, England's Spymaster, inventor of the Sandwich, and a member of the real Hellfire Club, (see appendix) as opposed to the Hellfire Club in the TV series "Stranger Things". With this Britain immediately declared war on Spain.

Britain sent a military expedition from India to take Manila in the Philippines and planned the expedition to capture Havana on the Island of Cuba in the West Indies, with the initial intention to then go on to take Louisiana.

With its deep water harbour, mile-long channel, and large Spanish shipyard, Havana was the most important port in the Spanish American colonies. It was also the base for a strong naval squadron and the rendezvous for treasure ships sailing between Spain and its South American colonies. The city was thought to be impregnable, with the guns of Fort El Morro able to fire on ships attempting to enter the harbour or any force attempting to take the fortress of Puntal.

The only chink in Havana's armour was the wooded La Cabañas ridge on the east side of the harbour, from which an attacker's guns could bombard the city. King Philip IV of Spain ordered the governor of Cuba, Don Juan de Prado, to fortify La Cabañas ridge, but Prado failed to do so. This proved to be a big mistake.

Siege of Havana

In 1762, the British launched an attack on Havana. They captured La Cabañas ridge and used its guns to bombard the city. After a two-month siege, Havana surrendered. The British occupation of Havana lasted for only 11 months, but it was a humiliating defeat for Spain.

The route taken by the assembled convoy took the dangerous Old Bahamas Channel. The approach with prevailing winds would be quick, and unlikely to meet other shipping that might warn the Spanish in Havana of the British approach, but it was incredibly dangerous to sail. In Havana, the British declaration of war against Spain was merely a rumour, the official notification from Spain having been on board a ship captured by a British warship.

Reports came in of the arrival of ships off Havana as Prado and the city dignitaries were in church, celebrating the feast of the Trinity. Prado's reaction was that it must be a passing fleet, until British troops began to land. Only then did the Spanish Governor, Del Prado, prepare his defenses, a clear indication of the complete surprise achieved by the British. A chain boom was placed across the mouth of the harbour and two ships of the line sunk behind the boom, with another added some days later (Neptuno, Asia and Europa).

After prolonged bombardment, by 17th July 1762, there were no Spanish guns left in action on the north-east bastion of El Morro castle, with only two in action elsewhere and the British commanders considered it was possible to begin an approach to the fortifications. At the end of July 1762, 3,188 British regular and American provincial troops, sent by General Amherst, arrived from America, providing a welcome reinforcement of healthy soldiers for Albemarle's army.

The British laid two mines to be fired; one under the outer bank or counterscarp of a 70-foot ditch, the other under the wall of the north-west bastion of El Morro Castle, with a storming party comprised 102 men from the 1st Royals, 129 Marksmen from various regiments and 50 men from the 90th Regiment. After 30 minutes of hand to hand fighting El

Morro Castle was taken, the Spanish commander, Captain Don Luis de Velasco being wounded.

A heavy bombardment of the city began at dawn on 11th August 1762. By 2pm on that day, Governor Prado concluded that further resistance was hopeless and Spanish officers were sent to the British lines under a flag of truce, seeking terms for the surrender of the city. Under the terms of capitulation, the Spanish surrendered to the British the city of Havana and all its environs, all military equipment, public records, merchant ships and warships in Havana harbour, public moneys and city warehouses with their contents. On 21st August 1762, the British fleet entered Havana Harbour and took control of 9 of the finest warships of the Spanish fleet and 100 merchant ships.

Prado and 11 other military and civil officials, exchanged for British prisoners, were sent back to Spain in shame. Their list of errors was long, having failed to fortify La Cabaña hill properly and abandoned it too quickly, having disabled the Spanish fleet by sinking three ships at the bay's mouth, and having surrendered the remaining fleet untouched rather than burning it. Also, they had not mounted any important counterassaults. But, probably most importantly, they had not removed the royal treasury before the surrender, and they had not evacuated the city, they simply had handed it over.

CHAPTER 4

WILLIAM NURENBURG & OAK ISLAND

Following the Siege of Havana and surrender to the British in 1762, the Manso family, understandably a little spooked by world events, arranged a shipment of their fortune to be deposited in London with a new Bank that was being created by John & Francis Baring, merchants the Manso family had been trading with for a long while. The shipment that was being transported in four transport ships under paid guard of British troops from the Royal Highlanders Regiment however split on reaching Nova Scotia, with one half of the fortune continuing to Plymouth under the escort of His Majesty's Ship - The Aldborough, who had left Quebec on the 10th of September.

The other two transports docked at Bridgewater Nova Scotia, where they unloaded their cargo into the hands of a Master James Crompton, and Master O'Hare, the captain and owner of a sloop called The Falmouth. Crompton, who knew the islands surrounding Nova Scotia, was tasked with hiding the part of the Manso fortune that had been extracted from the main cargo, somewhere in the surrounding islands. With the help from a American-British Engineer, William Nurenburg, on assignment from the Highlands Regiment, the treasure was successfully hidden in 1762 at Oak Island in what is now known as the Money Pit. William Nurenburg was a contemporary and exchanged letters with James-Watt, the Scottish inventor of the steam engine. Correspondence shows the interest in using steam engines to pump water out of mining tunnels. William was also possibly the leading expert of his day in mining tunnels that went under the sea, with experience at Botallack Tin Mine in Cornwall. One of the key clues in Oak Island that the tunnels were indeed man made is the discovery that coconut fibre was found in volume within the pits, a product not unusual for Cornish mining engineers to waterproof tunnels, and definitely not a local produce of Nova Scotia, or Cornwall for that matter, so it must have been shipped in.

Having the right resources to recover the buried fortune however required accurate planning plus a large team of labourers, transport and engineers. The first opportunity was aborted in 1771 due to plague being discovered amongst some of the Russian sailors engaged on that expedition, and it wasn't until 1796 when the expedition could be successfully re-attempted. Four ships could be diverted from the HMS Gangees Convoy who were preparing to ship prisoners of war captured on the islands of St Lucia, St Vincent and Grenada in the Caribbean back to the UK.

The four ships, with the labour and engineering skills to haul the hidden treasure out from the money-pit, had 4 weeks to sail from the Caribbean to Nova Scotia, onboard the chests, collapse the pit, re-supply and then re-join the convoy as it reached the auspices of Nova Scotia. We'll tell this tale in more detail in future chapters.

The 4 ships, including The London captained by Master William Robertson, and The New Adventure captained by James Ingate successfully extracted the fortune utilising the muscle of the French prisoners of war that they carried.

Built in 1785 in Dartmouth, England, The New Adventure was a British 18th century privateer. It was a 12-gun brigantine, commanded by Captain James Ingate. Ingate was a skilled and experienced sea captain, and he quickly made a name for himself as a successful privateer. In fact he was one of the most successful privateers in the history of the Royal Navy, and it is credited with capturing over 200 enemy vessels.

The New Adventure's first major success came in 1786, when it captured the French ship Le Fier Rodrigue. Le Fier Rodrigue was a 14-gun brigantine, carrying a valuable cargo of gold and silver. Her capture was a major coup for the British, and it helped to raise the New Adventure's profile.

The New Adventure continued to be successful in the years that followed. In 1787, it captured the French ship La Diane. La Diane was a 16-gun brigantine, carrying a cargo of slaves and was a major blow to the French slave trade. Captain Ingate was a close friend of William Robertson Master of The London, although in letters he sometimes referred to his friend as "John".

The treasure from Oak Island was successfully transported back to the UK, although one chest was lost from the London as it was being winched off the ship at Ilfracombe on the North Devon Coast. The London was likely then scuttled to hide evidence of the previous activities. To this day gold is still being washed up in Ilfracombe. William Nurenburg was present when the fortune was retrieved again in 1796 at Oak Island and lost his life when The London was scuttled at Ilfracombe.

CHAPTER 5

THE SINKING OF THE LONDON

The Lloyds Register lists a ship called the London, with Robertson as it's master in 1795. Built in Shoreham in 1764, The London, owned by James Mather (an investor in The Africa Company), was still described in good condition in 1795 having been fully refitted in 1788 and had a new deck installed in 1789. During the previous five years she had made voyages to Honduras and Venezuela where British and Dutch woodcutters exploited the valuable mahogany forests.

Records show she arrived February 10th 1796 at Portsmouth with seven other transports.

The Ilfracombe Port-Book, at Kew in London, gives the following account for 10th October 1796:

"Last evening, the London, of London, a transport, mastered by William Robertson from St Kitts, with French prisoners aboard, was unfortunately driven on-shore at the entrance of this harbour. upwards of 40 persons were drowned. The vessel was entirely lost!"

From the records at the Admiralty Office, Oct 22nd 1796: "Pursuant to an Act of Parliament, passed in the 26th year of the reign of his late Majesty, this is to give notice to the concerned, that information has been sent to this office that the Transport ship London, of London, whereof William Robertson was Master, bound from the Island of St Christopher's to Plymouth, was on the 9th instant, in tempestuous weather, unfortunately wrecked at the entrance of the harbour of Ilfracombe in the county of Devon."

Rewind three years. Fresh from the turmoil of her revolution, France declared war on Great Britain once again.

While Britain relied on her powerful navy, France resorted to what was known as, levée en masse - effectively mass conscription - to swell the ranks of her army. This remained the case even in her far-away colonies in the West Indies. The French released many slave labourers to fight against the British, often with free-born black officers leading them.

The spread of French Revolutionary ideals, with their motto of liberté, égalité and fraternité, posed a major threat to the social order of the Caribbean at the time, and indeed these ideals encouraged the spread of several revolts and uprisings amongst both the free and enslaved black populations, nowhere more dramatically than in Haiti, where the British Army would also become involved.

A French-born revolutionary, Victor Hugues, captured the island of Guadeloupe from Britain in 1794. He then declared an end to slavery and enlisted many former enslaved and free people of mixed race into the French Revolutionary army. Across the Caribbean, men of both African and European descent served in racially integrated military units that fought against Britain – which was still a slave-owning nation – on islands such as St Lucia, St Vincent and Guadeloupe.

A new expedition from Britain would soon change the course of the Caribbean war again. After many delays, Sir Ralph Abercromby arrived at Barbados on 17th March 1796, with orders to capture Guadeloupe and St. Lucia as his primary objectives.

On 26 May 1796, the French garrison holding Fort Charlotte on St Lucia surrendered to British forces commanded by Sir John Moore. They laid down their weapons and marched out of the fort and onto British ships. The terms of their surrender ensured that they would all be treated as prisoners of war, rather than as slaves.

Abercromby then sailed for St. Vincent, leaving some reinforcements at Grenada en route. Landing on St. Vincent on 8th June 1796, the following day he began a siege of the Vigie, a set of elevated fortifications to the east of Kingstown. Whilst many of the French Carib allies retreated in the face of this, the French generally held their ground. The British attempted to storm the French position at 14:00 hours and drove the enemy back from their outer defences, resulting in a French surrender at 17:00 hours.

On islands, such as St Lucia, St Vincent, Martinique and Grenada, they fought against the British. Some islands exchanged hands several times over the course of the conflict. The slaves-turned-soldiers were ultimately viewed as prisoners of War by the British, and were loaded onto large troop transport ships, to be taken across the Atlantic in convoys and into prisoner of war camps in Britain.

One such convoy, led by HMS Ganges, left St Kitts in July 1796. With 3,000 prisoners captured on the islands of St Lucia, St Vincent and Grenada. Official records show the London carrying, one Officer, Eight Serjeants, and Eleven Privates of the 66th Regt, and 106 French Prisoners - Black.

Gathering the convoy together had taken weeks. Despite poor weather blowing in, 3 of the transports including The London and one brigantine, The New Adventure, left Basseterre Bay before the whole convoy was assembled. Travelling in a convoy enabled all the ships to travel un-harassed, so there must have been strong reasons for the four ships to leave early!   The reason... they were off to Oak Island to retrieve the treasure that had been buried there in 1762, and this time they had a hold full of strong labourers, the black French soldiers. It was also important no one would tell tales of what they had retrieved at Oak Island.

Following the trade routes for slaves, sugar and molasses, they headed north, up the coast of the newly named, United States, but with a very different trade in mind. The gods were kind and the trade-winds pushed them ahead in urgent time, whilst HMS Gangees, and the rest of the convoy, were still trapped in safe-harbour under the protection of Basseterre

Bay.

James Crompton, originally the Master of the Falmouth, which had originally transported the treasure from Bridgewater to Oak Island, landed on the island with James Nurenberg, the mining engineer who had secured the tunnels to protect them from being plundered, alongside William Robertson and James Ingate. The black prisoners were used as the muscle to winch the heavy stones that changed the direction of the water or diverted seawater away from the main tunnels. This system was a replica of the acequia system of interconnected canals that can be found in the Balearics and other Spanish and South American villages. The puzzle was relatively simple, but the headstones had to be turned in the correct order, or the tunnels would flood.

Once the acequias had been successfully diverted, the main pit could be opened and the treasure removed. It would have taken at least 10 men to haul each chest to the surface, so it must have been very hard work for the black French soldiers who were tasked with this labour. They would have had to haul the chests to the surface and then transfer them to one of the four ships that were waiting offshore. If the French soldiers understood what they were hauling, they would have realized that they were unlikely to be allowed to live to tell the tale.

The operation was done with military precision and timing, enabling all four ships to rejoin the Gangees convoy just off Nova Scotia.

The Ganges convoy reached southern Ireland on the 22nd before splitting in two, with one group heading up St Georges Channel for a large prisoner-of-war camp at

Liverpool while the others made for Crookhaven Bay, behind Mizen Head in County Cork, where they anchored on September 26th. After replenishing supplies of fresh food and water they continued on towards Plymouth.

The four ships carrying the Manso treasure retrieved from Oak Island, however broke away, and made a sharp dash up the Bristol Channel towards Ilfracombe on the north Devon coast.

As they passed the southern tip of Ireland the south-south-westerly storms that had been battling the convoy got severely worse and continued to worsen as they headed up the Bristol Channel. One of the ships, The New Adventure, under Captain James Ingate, made better progress, arrived the evening before The London, and safely docked and unloaded before the other three arrived.

Something in the plan however had gone wrong. Although the pilot boats were happy to lead The London into the harbour, Robertson, the Captain of the London, refused and said he would tie up on a buoy outside the harbour breakwater, which was disastrous.

Or that was the story that was reported.

A shot was heard in the town from the London, but no answering shot was heard. Whether Robertson had received a signal from James Ingate of the New Adventure from shore, or even not received the signal he was expecting, he decided he would not go into harbour but tie up, hoping the storm would ease and he could make a break for open water.

According to a later account by a Captain Chiswell. The pilots - who help guide ships into difficult ports - rowed out to meet the boat, looking to guide her into Ilfracombe harbour.

They hollered over the rising wind. "Where are you from?

"From Hell, bound for damnation!" Robertson roared back, before dismissing their offers of help.

He tried to turn the ship on the buoy, but his ambitious manoeuvre failed, and the ship, with its prisoners chained in the hold, was dashed against the rocks at Rapparee Cove.

Captain Chiswell's account, held in the Ilfracombe Museum, was that The London contained five treasure chests, only four of which were recovered, but they then disappeared.

He described the cove, as "covered with the bodies of negroes", and recorded that the corpse of a young woman, "a naked lily fair", was also washed up.

Spanish coin, and bones, to this day are still often found in Rapparee cove.

However, there are some holes in the account by Captain Chiswell, who was in charge of the Pilot boat that went out to meet the London. In his account, admittedly written from memory after the event, he said "The valuables on board were contained in five chests - there was specie, Spanish dollars and doubloons! One of the chests was lost during the transfer from the ship, and was no doubt broken up at the bottom of the sea."

This would mean that there was time for the five chests to be transferred from the ship, before the ship was wrecked or scuttled on the rocks. Successfully winching 5 chests from a ship, violently breaking-up on the rocks, would be impossible. Even winching the chests from The London, moored on the buoy in rough seas, to another vessel, or a Pilot boat would have been a very desperate attempt, but it's clear from Chiswell's testimony a transfer of the treasure was planned and almost successfully executed, regardless of whether the ship was to be taken into harbour. It is most likely once the chests had been removed the ship was scuttled. Dead men tell no tales.

There was more to the story then was being reported! And there were others at the time who didn't believe the story being told.

Once the survivors from the London were safely ashore, The Royal Navy's Transport Board handed over responsibility for them to the Commissioners of Sick and Wounded Prisoners. Consequently on October 27th they sent a letter to Richard Allard, the civilian Agent-Contractor at the Admiralty prison at Stapleton, near Bristol, and this read "we acquaint you for your guidance that we have given direction to Mr Smith, Agent for Sick and Wounded at Biddeford to have a small vessel for the purpose of carrying between thirty and forty French prisoners from Ilfracombe, where they now are, to Bristol, and as they are chiefly, if not all, natives of the West Indies, we direct you to take care that they suffer as little as possible from the coldness of the season."

Stapleton had not originally been considered as a destination for any of the prisoners transported from the Ganges convoy, as prior to 1800 it possessed just one accommodation block, 256 feet long and 45 feet wide, and although the two floors were partitioned lengthways, it still only provided 4 narrow rooms. Although prisoners of war of various nationalities had been transferred to Stapleton since 1793, it was now already over-crowded. In Felix Farley's Bristol Journal it told it's readers that on Saturday December 3rd 1796 between thirty and forty Maroon prisoners from the West Indies were escorted by a troop of horse through this city to the prison at Stapleton. It is interesting that the paper called them "Maroons", as this was the term used to describe escaped slaves who had over the years established their own communities on various West Indian Islands. The original Maroons (from Cimarrones. the Spanish for mountaineers) had run away from their owners when the British took Jamaica from the Spanish in 1655, and in the interior mountains succeeded in maintaining their freedom and independence until 1796.

On December 4th the captives' personal details were written in the prison's General Entry Book and the 31 of them, all described as having been taken on St. Vincent and Grenada, were allocated numbers between 2681 and 2711. This relatively small intake was made up of 2710 and 2711, Colonel Commandant Heaurmaux of Fort Charlotte, St. Vincent, and his wife Marie-Jean, four French soldiers, 2681 Dumat; 2682 Lara; 2690 Charles; and 2706 Biardelle; II West Indian Mulattos, 2683 De Grave: 2685 La Combe; 2689 Oycuse: 2691 Balai: 2692 Joseph; 2694 Victor; 270 I Pierre; 2703 La Lainte; 2704 Baboud; 2702 Pepierre; and 2708 Bottreau; and 14 African Negroes, 2684 Sauchagrave; 2686 La Virtue: 2687 Hela; 2688 Felis; 2693 Dominique;

2695 Paschal; 2696 Lesperance; 2697 Andec; 2698 Jaques; 2699 Lindau; 2700 Timothee; 2702 Michael; 2705 Pierre; and 2709 Cadcaux.

The General Entry Book had a column to describe the "Quality" of the prisoners, in which was given their rank, profession or trade, and in this the Negroes and Mulatos were all described as "slaves" although it should be understood that this was a job description rather than their legal status, slavery in effect having been stopped in the British Isles by Lord Mansfield's court ruling of 1772. Of the original 31 survivors from the London, the French Colonel and his wife left on parole on December 8th 1796, to enter into gentile captivity in the company of other French officers and their families at Chippenham, while two of the French soldiers died in the prison hospital, 2706 Biradelle on February 15th 1797 and 2681 Dumat on April 3rd of the same year. The same fate also befell two Mulatos, 2694 Victor who passed away on December 22nd 1796 and 2701 Pierre on January 15th 1798. Colonel Heaurmaux was buried in St Mary's Church, Chippenham, December 8th 1797 with full military honors.

The written agreement between Britain and the French Republic which regulated the treatment of prisoners, enabled large groups of prisoners of war to be regularly repatriated to France throughout the conflict, either as sick or dying men, or in exchange for certain classes of British troops and seamen in French hands. The specially hired small brigs or schooners which plied between the two countries were known as Cartel Boats and prior to sailing the master of each had to obtain Admiralty approval, while the white flag of truce itself was sent directly from London. The prisoners from Stapleton were normally marched, or taken by wagon if invalids, around the outskirts of the city, across the Downs, and down to the Lamplighters Hall, an inn which still exists at Shirehampton where they rested prior to being taken across the Avon River on the ferry to Pill, from where the Cartel boats usually sailed for France.

As those arriving on The London had surrendered under Articles of Capitulation which required them to be repatriated to France, their incarceration, suffered on scanty rations in the unhealthy and overcrowded atmosphere of Stapleton Prison, was therefore relatively short. Consequently, the first two of these, 2697 Andee and 2700 Timothee, both Negroes and probably quite sickly, were discharged on October 12th 1797 and put aboard the Nancy cartel boat, which Captain Lewis had recently brought over from Swansea, and whose next port of call was to be La Rochelle in France. The remaining group of 23 who had been saved from the wreck of the London, by then comprising the two surviving French soldiers, 12 Negroes and 9 Mulatos, were initially released on January 19th 1798 and embarked on the 160 ton Smallbridge. a vessel which on January 7th Lieutenant Clements at Plymouth had ordered Captain Jackson to sail for King Road, at the mouth of the Bristol Avon, its final destination being recorded in Felix Farley's Bristol Journal as the French port of Brest, in Brittany.

The London sank before the Burial of Drowned Persons Act of 1808 was passed, which required shipwrecked bodies to be buried in consecrated ground.

However, even before this law was passed, shipwreck victims were often given decent burials when possible. So, why were the bodies of the London's victims not buried properly, as Captain Chiswell claimed?

There are a few possible explanations.

Was it because it may have been difficult to get a priest to the scene to perform a burial.

Were the bodies so badly dismembered or decomposed by the time they were found, making it difficult to give them a proper burial.

Some people have claimed that black people were not given Christian burials in North Devon at the time because they were viewed as heathens. However, this is unlikely, as North Devon was known for its religious devotion. Additionally, although Bideford had ties to the slave trade, there was also a strong anti-slavery movement in the area.

The sinking of the London in Rapparee Cove 200 years ago was a tragedy that unfolded at the hands of the sea, a ruthless captain, and the jagged rocks of the cove.

The bodies of the victims were reportedly strewn across the beach, and some locals claimed that they saw Robertson and his crew looting the ship's cargo as the survivors struggled to escape.

The sinking of the London was a horrific event, and it is a reminder of the dangers of the sea and the cruelty of human beings.

The legend of the London came alive again in 1997, when a

young boy walking along the beach at Rapparee found what turned out to be a human bone. More started turning up, so a dig was organised to find out what was underneath the sand.

Sure enough, more human remains were found, along with leg irons, coins and manacles. There were calls in St Lucia for the remains of the men, seen there as freedom fighters, to be returned. African groups demanded that they be sent back to Africa as they felt they were slaves from the continent.

Gold coins continue to be found to this day around Ilfracombe. One rare coin sold at auction in 2022 for approximately 700,000 USD.

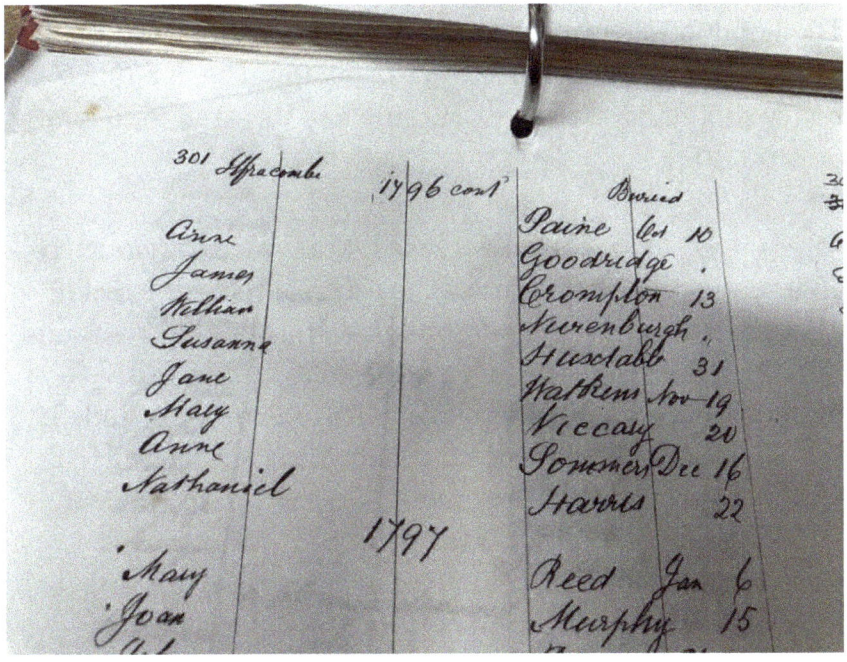

Ilfracombe Church Record

William Nurenburg didn't survive the scuttling of The London and was buried in Holy Trinity Church, Ilfracombe on the 13th of October 1796, curiously alongside a Captain James Crompton, the Master of The Falmouth who both must have also been on board The London. Captain William Robertson, The Master of the London, survived and escaped without any charge, albeit under suspicion, becoming Master of a ship called The Hope that was again shipwrecked or scuttled in 1797 and Robertson again surviving that tragedy as well. The insurance was paid out on both The London and The Hope. However, it seems despite his "poor turn of luck", he was living well in rooms at the Ye Olde Mitre by the London Diamond and Jewellery area of Hatton Garden, before sailing for Fortaleza, Brazil in 1801.

The London was insured by the Royal Exchange Assurance Corporation, a British insurance company. The insurance policy should have covered the ship and its cargo for a total of £100,000.

After the London was shipwrecked, the insurers conducted an investigation to determine the cause of the shipwreck. They did not believe the reasons given for the shipwreck and initially refused any pay-out until a more in-depth investigation could be carried out. The insurers concluded that they were not liable for the shipwreck, suspecting foul play, but they agreed to pay out £35,000 to the owners of the London to protect future trade with the Royal Africa Company, one of the most powerful companies in the British Empire. This was a fraction of the ship's value, but it was a significant amount of money at the time. The owners of the London were however not happy with the insurers' decision, and they appealed the decision to the Court of Chancery. The court ruled in favour of the owners of the London, and they were awarded the additional £65,000.

CHAPTER 6

THE MANSO TONTINE

A Tontine is the name of an early system for raising capital in which a family may make a deposit on behalf of a family, syndicate or group, or individuals pay into a common pool of money; in turn they receive dividends based on their share of returns from investments made with the pooled money. As members of the group died, they were not replaced with new investors so the proceeds were divided among fewer and fewer members. The longer you live—and the fewer fellow investors who remain living—the larger your annual payment. The last investor alive would collect the entire dividend. When all the investors died, the tontine ended, and the issuer would retain the capital. This might be a bank or Government or a private institution. If it was a family Tontine the capital could be reinvested into a new Tontine based on the relatives of the surviving member of the first Tontine. This way the family capital is never lost and transverses the generations.

In 1775, English freemasons used a tontine to finance the first Freemasons' Hall (the Freemasons' Tontine) in Great Queen Street, London. Today this building—called the

United Grand Lodge of England (UGLE)—houses more than 200,000 member freemasons.

The Tontine Coffee House, the forerunner of the New York Stock Exchange, was one of New York City's busiest hubs for buying and selling stocks and transacting business deals.

Tontines have fallen from favour in more recent times in the US and UK but in Europe tontines are regulated under the Directive 2002/83/EC of the European Parliament and tontines are still common in France.

Tontines, even those reinvested over centuries have the benefit of the capital being protected and have moved into modern times through automation with blockchain.

Of course, one of the traditional challenges of the Tontine was that the fewer people who survived, the more share the others got. This has caused many family feuds and grisly murders. On the plus side these Tontine murders have produced some interesting literature and TV! The plot of the Agatha Christie murder mystery "4:50 From Paddington", with Miss Marple, is based on a tontine will. In The Wrong Box, a novel by Robert Louis Stevenson, the object is to conceal the death of one of the last two tontine investors. The novel was the basis of the 1966 film The Wrong Box starring Michael Caine, Peter Sellers, Dudley Moore and Peter Cook. Even in an episode of The Simpsons, Grampa and Mr. Burns enter into a tontine during World War II, involving a treasure of antique paintings stolen from a German castle. When the two of them become the only surviving members, they compete for the rights to the prize…. And of course, we can't forget the Bugs Bunny cartoon The Fair-Haired Hare (1951). Bugs Bunny and Yosemite Sam sue each other over a house. However, they are forced to share ownership and are bound to a tontine, the judge declaring "and in the event that one should pass on, the other shall inherit the land fully." Yosemite Sam spends the rest of the cartoon trying to find inventive ways to dispose of Bugs.

It could be seen that a tontine is a bet that one person will outlive the other, and although it may encourage those with other shares to reduce the competition, for the family members who benefitted from the one share in their family group, keeping that member alive, was tempered by the spectre of the nominee's death, an event which would instantly render a tontine share worthless.

Tontines are also used as a way to get around succession law. For example, France's succession law is notorious for its principle of forced heirship, whereby children are the reserved heirs of their parents. Therefore, on the death of the first parent, the children have a protected right to inherit part of the estate which they will share with the surviving spouse. Where succession is disputed or fortune might be claimed by a large number of claimed heirs, the tontine will protect the capital to only those the family want to inherit. However, what is does also mean is that the capital never disappears, so would-be claimants, if they could successfully challenge ownership, even after hundreds of years could make it on the rolls of the new tontine when the last man or woman standing on the old had died.

In the late Middle Ages tontines became widespread in Europe as a financing tool of the royal courts. Because levying taxes was often out of the question, European monarchs borrowed, predominantly via tontines, to fund their internecine wars.

At the height of their popularity in the 1900s, tontines represented almost two-thirds of the insurance market in the United States and accounted for more than 7.5% of the nation's wealth. By 1905, there were an estimated nine million active tontine policies in the U.S.

The tontine could be managed by a bank or a government or a private institution. Sometimes the demise of the tontine based on last beneficiary was replaced with naming of the death of a public figure and at which time the tontine would be wound up and final dividend paid to the remaining beneficiaries. King George the Third was named in the English Government Tontine of 1789 who lived long for the benefit of those who invested, however the Irish Tontine of 1777 named Marie Antoinette, who we all know lost her head.

A French recurring tontine created by William Paterson (Founder of Bank of England) may still be paying out yearly income to some Manso descendants, or at least named beneficiaries of the tontine funded by the Oak Island and Manso fortunes. The tontine would be re-issued multiple times with new surviving beneficiaries. There are references on other internet pages to bank account numbers. These more closely resemble a Tontine account. With the death of Queen Elizabeth of the United Kingdom in 2022, the longest reigning UK monarch of 70 years, although not a beneficiary, several tontines will likely be tied to the date of death and will now be cancelled and re-designed with new beneficiaries.

A recurring tontine of this age will have moved into the modern world as proof of the beneficiary still being alive is paramount. A tontine custodian administrator must maintain an effective method of identifying which members have died and which have survived. Today biometric technologies are often suggested as solutions. For example, payouts will be withheld until members log in to a computer or mobile phone application and positively identify themselves as being alive (e.g., using facial recognition technology). Because such biometric technologies are imperfect they may be backed up by periodic queries to official government death records. The current beneficiaries will therefore have access to an online system that will identify them, provide statements and enable pay-out. All this leaves a data trail.

THE OAK ISLAND CODE

CHAPTER 7

THE TONTINE OF 1882

There has always been speculation that His Royal Highness the Prince of Wales (later King Edward VII) had an interest in some part of the Manso Fortune. It is suspected that a private rolling tontine was being administered by Sir Frederick Johnstone, 8th Baronet of Westerhall. Sir Johnstone was a close friend of His Royal Highness and had a playboy reputation as a racehorse owner and womaniser, being named as a co-respondent in the divorce case involving Sir Charles Mordaunt and his wife Harriet (1870) in which the prince was also called to give evidence.

In January 1882 His Royal Highness visited Bradgate Park, the seat of Lord Stamford. The estate was previously held by Sir John Grey, the first husband of Elizabeth Woodville, who afterwards became Queen of King Edward IV. Lady Jane Grey was born here. Jane was the Tudor Queen who ruled for just nine days before being executed on a charge of treason by King Henry VIII.

Although the visit was mainly promoted as a pheasant shooting trip around Bradgate and Groby, it was also a meeting of the shareholders of a tontine. The invited shareholders included The Prince of Wales, Lord Stamford, Viscount Newport, the Earl of Lathom, Colonel Kenyon Slaney, Colonel sir Henry Halford, Lord Ormathwaite, Earl de Grey, Sir Frederick Johnstone, Mr Trelawney, Mr de Lisle, Colonel Teesdale, The Earl of Hardwicke, Mr Christopher Sykes M.P, Colonel Lloyd and Lord Forester. There were other shareholders who were present at the dinner, but not the shoot. Edward John Phelps who subsequently became US ambassador to The Court of St James's was representing investment from the US government, The agent of Barings Bank in Buenos Aires, Nicholas Bouwer, Joseph Quintero, US consul to Belgium and Costa Rica, and Ernesto Pacelli a representative of Vincenzo Gioacchino Raffaele Luigi Pecci, Pope Leo XIII.

Tontine Dinner at Bradgate Park

As previously explained, a tontine pays a regular income to the members of the tontine based on a large joint investment where following the death of an individual member, the deceased share passes to the surviving members. In practice, it wasn't as crude as it sounds. Like most financial instruments, tontines became ever-more sophisticated, with hedges and sub-shares and derivatives. One feature of the larger tontine investments was to nominate a very "public" life as the one on which the investment depended before being settled between the remaining "living" beneficiaries, on that public life's death. It also protected individual members, nervous that their own premature death may have advantaged the others with their share. This particular tontine had previously been linked to the death of the Earl of Beaconsfield, Benjamin Disraeli, the only Jewish man in the history of Britain to have held the post of Prime Minister, who had died the previous April. This meeting of the shareholders was to re-issue the tontine, nominate the beneficiaries and to link to the life of a new public individual.

Another non-related tontine, known as the Irish Tontine, had been linked to Marie Antionette of France who at the age of 21 would have been thought to have a long life ahead of her and would have seemed a safe bet. Unfortunately she was imprisoned during the French Revolution with the threat of the guillotine. A plot was hatched by the Irish backers to free the Queen and bring her to Ireland. Not for political reasons, but to protect their investment. Unfortunately for Marie Antionette she was not rescued and lost her head. Members of the Irish Tontine who were expecting to live the longest however lost their advantage.

The meeting at Bradgate was behind closed doors after dinner and after the ladies had retired. The only reference to that conversation refers to an unusual name. Signorina Evangelina Bottero of Mantua who was referred as taking a doctors degree in natural sciences. It is likely that she was named as the new public figure of the rolling tontine. Although Signorina Evangelina was not a high-profile public figure, it was not unusual to place that role on a young woman with an expected long life expectancy. It is also possible she was recommended from a Papal representative from the University where she had studied. One of the attendees at the shareholder meeting was Mr Edwin de Lisle, representative of the family Manso.

Signorina Evangelina Bottero of Mantua died in 1950 and the remaining Tontine shareholders would have re-issued in the following year or two. The new public figure would very likely have been Queen Elizabeth II whose coronation was in 1952, a young woman with a potential long life expectancy, as there was intense nationalism in Britain around at that time. But who were the shareholders? With the death of Queen Elizabeth II in 2022 the rolling tontine would be re-issued in 2023. The shareholders will undoubtedly include international government interests on both sides of the Atlantic, and within the Caribbean as well as private shareholders and could possibly include Church representation. The Manso family share should be held by someone representing a branch of that family, however whoever holds that share now may not have the Manso heirs as their primary beneficiary.

Clarification: Queen Elizabeth would not be a beneficiary, or have any financial interest, only the person on who's death the tontine bet would be redeemed and re-issued by the tontine's shareholders.

CHAPTER 8

THE CHAMBERCOMBE MANOR CONNECTION

Chambercombe Manor dates back to 1066 so, for some, it comes as no surprise that its ghosts are still in residence and often let their presence be known. A remote location, 900 years of history, legends of wreckers, smugglers, hidden bodies and an executed Queen of England -- Chambercombe Manor has seen it all. Mentioned in the Domesday book, the house was commissioned by William the Conqueror. It was owned by the Champernon family from around 1162 until the early 16th century, and then became the property of Henry, Duke of Suffolk, the father of Lady Jane Grey.

Chambercombe Manor boasts an eerie secret chamber that was uncovered in 1865 during renovation work. The then tenant, baffled yet intrigued, concluded that there must be a hidden room next door to what is now known as Lady Jane's room. He discovered a large, rather grand room with a four-poster bed surrounded by a red curtain in the centre. But the grimmest discovery was the skeleton of a young woman lying in the bed.

The skeleton is thought to be that of a young woman who was murdered in the chamber centuries ago. Her identity and the circumstances of her death remain a mystery, but her presence continues to haunt the manor.

The secret chamber is now open to visitors, and it is one of the most popular attractions at Chambercombe Manor. Visitors can learn about the history of the chamber and the mystery surrounding the young woman's skeleton.

The skeleton is said to be that of Kate whose father, William Oatway, was known as a smuggler and wrecker in the 1700s and was a tenant of Chambercombe. Legend has it that the ship Kate was travelling on, The Granada, back from Ireland was purposefully drawn ashore by lanterns tied to horses' tails, which the captain of the ship mistook to be other ships in the harbour bobbing up and down, with the light mimicking a stern lantern. The survivors were clubbed to death as they tried to come ashore. One lady in a silk gown whose face had been disfigured by the rocks and by beating was William Oatway's own daughter.

During the long period of the 18th century Continental Wars, the shortage of able-bodied men for home service, coupled with official corruption, allowed smugglers and wreckers to do very much as they liked, and so they carried on their job in open defiance of the law. However, one precaution they did take was to make villagers face the wall when they approached with their contraband. Then if an individual smuggler was arrested later, the villagers could truthfully swear that they had seen nothing, for hearing was not evidence.

> 'Them that ask no questions isn't told a lie,
> Watch the wall, my darling, while the gentlemen go by'
> (Kipling: "The Smuggler's Song")

The sight of a ship foundering would bring the nearby population to the beach, and before long, using pick-axes and hatchets the ship would be dismembered and any goods on it, carried away.

The law in those days deemed it illegal to claim salvage from a wrecked ship if anyone was left alive on it. The law was ingrained in the cultural history of the people of England having been in place since 1275:

> "Where a man, dog or a cat escape quick out of a ship, that such ship nor barge, nor anything within them, shall be adjudged a wreck" - Statute of Westminster

Therefore, the law virtually condemned any survivors found to death! Wreckers would stop survivors making it ashore, or would actively hold them down with poles until they drowned. There are many stories of lanterns tied to horses tails in order to lure the ships onto the rocks, it may have happened, but it was certainly in the folk law and newspapers of the day.

Smuggling and wrecking was common in north Devon in the 18th and early 19th centuries. Smugglers were known to have used Lee, Ilfracombe, Rapparee Cove, Watermouth Cove and Morte. Some of the smuggling operations were clearly considerable; in 1785 a 96 gallon cask of rum was found at Watermouth Cove and in 1801 224 gallons of gin and 164 gallons of brandy were found on the foreshore near Ilfracombe. It seems that everyone from the town and surrounding area were involved; in 1783 all the Ilfracombe pilot boats were suspected of smuggling and one, the Cornwall, was seized and cut up into three parts. It is therefore not surprising that the pilot boats that went out to assist the The London before it was scuttled in Ilfracombe were suspected of being involved of assisting Captain Robertson to unload the treasure chests.

In 1888, in an article on smuggling, a local 'old man' claimed that when he was a boy, there was a smuggler's tunnel from Hele Beach to an old well at Chambercombe. Another article from 1933 quoted Nathaniel Lewis, who lived in Hele, as saying that the tunnel led to Rapparee Cove. In 1976, Lilian Wilson wrote that the tunnel, now collapsed, led to a ledge high up in Samson's Cave, accessible only by ladder. There is also said to have been a tunnel from Watermouth Cove to the Castle, and the Tunnels in Ilfracombe are said to have originally been a smugglers cave. There is also a legend of a tunnel from Chambercombe Manor to Hele beach.

The most infamous smuggler in north Devon was Thomas Benson, who in 1747 became MP for Barnstaple. The following year he was granted a lease on the Island of Lundy and entered into contract with the Government to carry convicts abroad. However, he landed them on Lundy instead to run his smuggling operation.

He became overconfident and was fined for smuggling and stripped of his office. He didn't pay and his lands in Bideford were seized. To recover his losses he persuaded the Captain of the Nightingale to fire it for the insurance, but the plan was discovered and he fled to Portugal and then on to Brazil, Taquari. The captain was tried and executed in 1754.

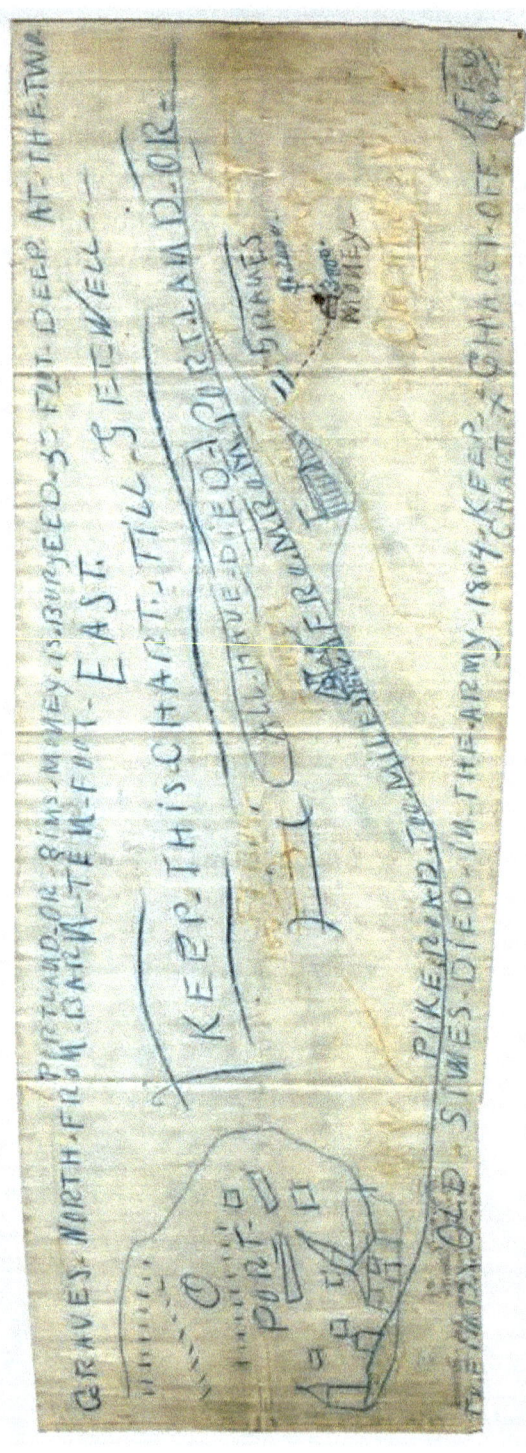

CHAPTER 9

THE PORTLAND OREGON CONNECTION

The map of a buried treasure in Portland, Oregon (see across) surfaced in the posthumous papers of judge Everett Smith. The map was in the possession of this son, Iriving D. Smith, until his death. With no living relatives his papers went to the court which gave the map to the Oregan Historical Society.

John Hampton Sims Jr, known as "old man Sims" was the son of John Hampton Sims Snr and Mary Brown Sims. He studied at Yale and became a Physician in the town of Woodville USA where he was raised. During the US Civil War he was promoted from a Lieutenant in Company D of the 21st Mississippi Infantry Regiment in 1861 to Lt. Col. and commander of the regiment in 1863. Although seriously wounded in the Battle of Cedar Creek, Virginia and being hospitalised, he rallied only to be killed on October 19, 1864.

Whilst laying wounded in the army hospital he is alleged to have told a story of Spanish pirate treasure that had been entrusted to him by a friend and patient of his, José Agustín Quintero, a Cuban Born in Havana to a Cuban tobacco planter named Antonio Quintero and an English woman named Anna Woodville. He studied at Colegio de San Cristóbal, Harvard University and had been a spy for the

South during the civil war. The money, gold coin, was said to be Jose' mothers. Anna Woodville was a descendant of the English Woodville's whose name crops up everywhere during the tales of the Manso family. The house once owned by the Woodville family at Ilfracombe used to smuggle some of the Manso fortune, Chambercome Manor in 1796; the location of the shareholders meeting at Bradgate Park once the seat of the Woodville's and was where Jose joined dinner with the other shareholders to discuss the 1882 Tontine. The fact that Woodville was the name of the town where Sims was a physician must surely just be coincidence. The story was apparently told to another injured soldier, a Private James M Dancer, from Crystal Springs, who drew the map from Old Man Sim's oral description. Whether the money had been buried by Jose Quintero or John Sims was not clear. We do know that James Dancer documented the location from Sim's description. There was also reference, to another person named Jonathan Knight but how that relates we are currently unsure.

Although the map shows "money" rather than gold or treasure is not unusual. The money buried in 1862 was unlikely to have been bank notes as at that time notes were seen as unreliable, so it was most likely gold coin, Golden Beavers if local or Spanish Coin if not. Both Oregon and California had successfully rebelled against federal authority during the Civil War. Specifically, they defied the 1862 Legal Tender Act by refusing to accept greenbacks as legal tender and essentially nullified the Act with impunity.

Since gold was more common on the West Coast than the East, Californians and Oregonians were weary of greenbacks. In April 1863 the California legislature adopted a Specific Contracts Act, clarifying that contracts entered on the basis of specie were only enforceable in specie. Finally the California state government refused to accept greenbacks in payment of taxes.

Oregon quickly followed California. For years gold had been the exclusive Oregon currency. Shortly after the San Francisco merchants' agreement, those in Salem and Portland followed suit. Portland merchants also circulated a blacklist of residents and businesses that tried to settle bills with greenbacks. Finally, the state's Supreme Court ruled that it was unconstitutional to accept greenbacks for tax payments. Therefore it is almost certain the money on the map would have been in the form of gold.

The Great Plank Road, also known as the Pike Road, was constructed in 1856 to connect agricultural communities in the Tualatin Valley to Portland. It was paved with sixteen-foot, three-inch-thick wooden planks and offered a significant improvement over the previous dirt road, which was often muddy and impassable in adverse weather conditions.

The Pike Road is now Portland Canyon Road. It begins in Goose Hollow, near the Vista Bridge, where Jefferson Street transitions into Canyon Road. The road then climbs up the canyon behind the Vista Ridge Tunnels, where the Sunset Highway (Route 66) goes over Sylvan Hill. Slightly west of Sylvan, an interchange with modern Canyon Road (Oregon Route 8) continues southwest into Beaverton. Two blocks west of Cedar Hills Boulevard, at the junction with Hocken Road, the contemporary road name changes to Tualatin Valley Highway ("TV Highway"). However, the original plank road continued farther west.

The Great Plank Road was a vital transportation link for the early development of Portland and the Tualatin Valley. It allowed farmers to transport their produce and livestock to market more efficiently and helped to fuel the growth of the region's economy. The road also played an important role in the movement of people and goods between Portland and the Willamette Valley.

Some researchers have placed the location of the gold somewhere near to what is now Portland Zoo, which had previously been a farm with some characteristics similar to those described on the map. However, the data picked up from local news groups have moved beyond that location and are currently focused around Beaverton and even as far out as Hazeldale. The key being the reference to the orchards.

So what value is this part of the treasure. If it was confederate bank notes then the value is very little. $6000 in raw gold may be worth $400,000 today. However, if the coins are those known in pioneer days as Beaver Money, gold coins minted in Oregon in 1849, then 8 years ago a $5 coin was sold for just under $300,000. So, imagine having 1,200 of those! ($360,000,000). And, if it was Spanish coin, depending on rarity, each coin's value could be higher still.

CHAPTER 10

THE FLORIDA CONNECTION

After the US civil war, a Cuban named Juan Gonzales settled in Shell Creek near Lettuce Lake in DeSoto County. There are a number of different stories that relate to Juan Gonzales, most describing him as an old pirate from the crew of Jose Gaspar or Gasparilla, a famous Florida based pirate. The local story is that Gasparilla had been tipped off, of the voyage route that one of the ships carrying gold bullion that the United States had paid Napoleon for the Louisiana Purchase would be taking. He took the ship. This is legend, and unfortunately, we cannot find evidence of this. What we do know however is this.

William Augustus Bowles, born in Maryland, during the revolutionary war was loyal to the King, stationed in Philadelphia. His regiment was sent to Pensacola with the aim to attack the southern colonies, but he was not impressed with the resources available or his commanding officer and resigned his commission. He headed inland and lived with the Upper and Lower Creeks, Cherokee and Miccosukee Indians, learning their language and customs and married an Indian princess. At the end of the revolutionary war he went to Nassau and made friends with the Governor Lord Dunmore who in 1788 sent William Bowles to London with some of the Indian Chiefs. Whilst in London the British, with Bowles, devised a plan to try and capture Florida and turn it into a British Protectorate as a Creek Indian Nation to harass and infiltrate the Spanish in the south. In 1791 he landed in Florida and took Saint Marks. However, he was doubled crossed by the Spanish who said they would negotiate and was imprisoned for 8 years in Seville and then Manilla. In 1799 he escaped back to London. England and Spain were now officially at War. The British still liked the plan to capture Florida, but this time Bowles would be better supported by the British and negotiations with Spain were off the table.

Between 1799 and 1802 William Bowles secured large tracts of land in Florida, especially around the coast and named it the Muskogee nation with himself as Director General. He was able to attract a large number of Privateers, mostly ex-British officers from the Royal Navy who, given Letters of Marque from the nation of Muskogee, would be enabled to attack Spanish ships. At one point it was estimated that he had over 300 Privateers off the Florida coast. The most influential Privateer was Richard Powers, captain of the Muskogee Micco who alongside the other privateers controlled the West Coast of Florida. Richard Powers centred his fleet at Apalachee Bay, Cedar Key and Tampa Bay, ideal harbours to attack Spanish ships heading along the West Florida coast heading for Pensacola and New Orleans. Then, in 1802, the British signed a treaty with Spain and the Letters of Marque were no longer valid. Many of the privateers left and William Bowles was captured and died in prison. Cedar Key however continued as a base for pirates.

In 1803 the Louisiana Purchase was completed and New Orleans, that had previously been heavily restricted with whom could trade there, was now open to all trade, becoming a Pirate friendly port. One pirate who based himself just outside New Orleans was Jean Laffite who had a base at Barataria and Cedar Key on the Florida west coast. One of Jean Laffite's pirates was Louis Michael Aury, previously a French Naval Officer, who first sailed from Cedar Key, but following an argument they parted ways. Aury moved to Amelia Island, on the east coast near the Georgia border, in around 1808 and was smuggling slaves into Georgia.

At this time Simon Bolivar was leading an uprising in Venezuela against the Spanish. By 1817 the revolution was starting to falter as the Spanish pressed more and more troops into the Caribbean. Bolivar hired Louis Michael Aury to lead an attack on the Florida east coast by sea, supported by a US mercenary army from the north, with the intention of causing enough concern with the Spanish that they would divert some of their troops. In September 1817 Aury arrived at Amelia Island which he knew well and attacked the recently built fort, continuing to use it as his base. He successfully continued his piracy, smuggling slaves and goods taken from the ships travelling up the east coast into Georgia. Off Fernandina, he captured a Spanish slave ship and illegally sold its cargo of 95 enslaved Africans to a Georgia citizen for $60,000.

In September 1817 Aury captured an English ship, The Edward, under Master Germain, transporting a shipment from Havana to London. This shipment originally destined to Barings Bank will most likely have been from the Manso family. On 23 December of 1817 the USS John Adams sailed into port commanded by Commodore J.D. Henley and Major

James Bankhead. They arrested Aury but could not hold him for lack of evidence.

Aury and his crew sailed back around to Cedar Key and then on to Old Providence Island which became his new base. On route to Providence, they sailed down to Shell Creek near Lettuce Lake in DeSoto County in order to bury their treasure because US warships patrolling the area had become too threatening to risk losing their fortune. Aury intended to come back for it but died in 1821. One loyal member of Aury's crew was left with the buried treasure but on being informed of his death decided to recover the chests. The story goes that he asked for help from two ranchers to help him, but by the time they arrived, he too had passed away. The story became local legend and was later printed in both local papers and the Illustrated London News in the 1870's. Aury's treasure is located somewhere around the waters of Lettuce Lake, a wide spot in a tributary of the Peace River.

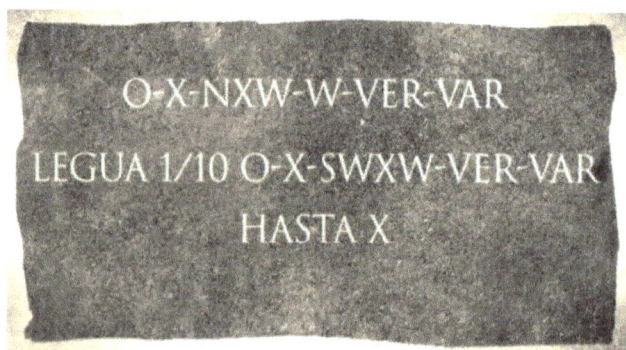

In the newspapers there were references to an old copper plate with a reference to where the treasure was buried. Although we believe there is treasure to be found here, the copper plate is likely a hoax. But to leave no stone unturned we have investigated the code etched into the plate to see what we can make out and have thrown some cryptographic ciphers at it. One outcome strangely suggested a cipher key based on the seating plan from the Forum Theatre in Billingham, Stockton, which suggested 7 pig pens in a line. Unfortunately that theatre wasn't built until 1967! Unless the theatre was built on a plan of a much older theatre. Another outcome was a pattern from canonical atom numbers but we can't imagine Aury being a master of computational chemistry! So that is out. One outcome, possibly our favourite, is that the code is based around the Miccosukee calendar. If so it describes days of the year, not directions. Whether this relates to tides when landmarks would be visible is a possibility as that method of direction has been used elsewhere, but all languages do not all follow the same structure as English or Spanish. There are over 7000 languages in the world today, and back in the early 1800's there were lots more. The language we speak shapes the way we think. Take one example, credit Lera Boroditsky, from the aboriginal people of Pormpuraaw, west edge of Cape York. They don't use terms like left and right they use cardinal directions, North, South, East and West. You don't say hello, you say which way are you going? So, throughout your day, every person you meet you have to report your heading direction. You couldn't get passed, hello, if you didn't know which way you were going.

We also don't record time in the same way. In England we organise a series of words or pictures from left to right when we talk about time. In Pormpuraaw they don't have that concept of left or right. When you sit them facing south they organised time from left to right. When sat facing north they organised time from right to left. Facing East, time comes towards the body. So what if this copper plate cipher was based on the Miccosukee calendar? Then we need to truly understand their language. Although it doesn't make sense to us, apparently we need to face West, black water, wait for the moon and the Ants will take us there. We are afraid that's not much use, unless you can read something into that that we haven't spotted. We will keep trying!

CHAPTER 11

MARY BUCKINGHAM

This location, unfortunately name unknown at this time in conjunction with a family name - Mary Buckingham. This photograph, held within a London bank archive has a reference to a tontine account in the name of Mary Buckingham. Who was she and where is this place? This could be one of the strongest clues to the location of the missing fortune. Currently however we draw a blank.

CHAPTER 12

SO WHERE ELSE COULD THE TREASURE BE?

YAGUAJAY

In the area surrounding the hacienda purchased in July 1697 from Gonzales de la Cruzy Crespo (Jose), a priest who was a close family friend and who had baptised Isabel Hernandez de Medina y Vida in 1671. Letters between Bartolome and Doctor Esteban de Fuente from Bayano, hint that he was worried of cimarronaje, slaves running away surrounding Yaguajay and joining a Palenques, a community of runaway slaves. Worried about them finding refuge in the cave with leaf bats.

Yaguajay, today

MARLOW, ENGLAND

The Manso de Contreras family have had long ties with England. The estate of Stag Hill was originally granted to the Manso de Contreras family by King Henry VIII in 1540. The family built a large mansion on the estate, which was known as Stag Hill House. The house was demolished in the 18th century, but the estate remained in the family until the 19th century.

The Manso family granted land for the building of both St. Peter's Church and Marlow College, important landmarks of the town, which are still standing today. They also funded the Old Bridge of Marlow before it was replaced in 1832. The original bridge was 210 feet long and 20 feet wide, built of stone with five arches. They are a testament to the generosity and philanthropy of the Manso de Contreras family.

CAYO SANTA MARIA

A strong room is reputedly buried on Cayo Santa Maria. seis y cuatro Vara, debajo del agua "beneath the water". Likely a cave that could only be accessed from under water. Five pearl diving slaves were brought from Margarita to the Manso estate in 1707. Pearl divers (pictured above) were known for being able to hold their breath underwater for long periods of time.

TONTINE – FINANCIAL INSTRUMENT

A rolling tontine is an investment linked to a living person which provides an income for as long as that person is alive. Such schemes originated as plans for governments to raise capital in the 17th century and became relatively widespread in the 18th and 19th centuries. A French tontine created by William Paterson (Founder of Bank of England) now regulated by the Directive 2002/83/EC of the European Parliament may still be paying out yearly income to some Manso descendants but most likely the interests have now passed to non-family members. The tontine was re-issued multiple times with new surviving beneficiaries. There are references on other internet pages to bank account numbers. These more closely resemble a Tontine account.

COVENT SANTA CLARA, HAVANA

Bartolome arranged for his daughters; María Isabel del Santísimo Sacramento, María Dolores de la Resurrección and María Manuela de San, to hide five chests at the convent. Three chests were later shipped to England, on El Titán under Master Tomas Morrison, accompanied by Jose Manso de Contreras y Perez del Prado. Two chests are unaccounted for.

ISLA MARGARITA

Year 1704 - Santa Rosa de la Eminencia, Margarita, where Francisca, a family relative, emigrated to in 1585, and where other members of the family held positions within local government, including Isla Margarita's representation in Spain.

TREGADILLET, CORNWALL

The treasure chests unloaded before the London was scuttled were likely taken through tunnels to Chambercombe Manor before being transported to The Square and Compass, now known as the Elliot Arms, Tregadillett, Cornwall, a public house where French Officer prisoners of war were held on parole. The French Officers formed a branch of Freemasonry here, 'The Lodge Consulate Maconne'. Local legend has it the freemason regalia on the walls of the pub give clues to where local treasure has been buried. It may be co-incidence but the French officer Colonel Commandant Heaurmaux of Fort Charlotte, St. Vincent, and his wife, survivors from The London, following a brief spell on parole in Chippenham requested a transfer to Tregadillet. Why?

TAQUARI

Investigating large transport of "supplies" from the Manso Estate to remote town of Taquari (Taquarey) what is now within state of Rio Grande do Sul, Brazil. Transport arranged by Snr H Akwa,(Aqua) a colonist originally from Neu-Kolonie in Russia, a new town of Wolgadeutsche (Volga Germans)

BARINGS BANK

Multiple shipments were made to London Banks. Barings was likely to have taken a deposit in 1762 that helped underwrite the creation of the bank and instrumental in the United States government's purchase of Louisiana from Napoleon Bonaparte in 1803. This doubled the size of the United States. After an initial payment of $3 million in gold, Barings Bank went bust in 1995 when a young trader, Nick Leeson, lost $1.3 billion of the bank's money in risky derivatives and unauthorized derivatives trades. The venerable bank collapsed, and Leeson spent four years in a Singapore prison.

PUERTO RICO

Year 1710 - Report of a heavy transport of seven chests from the Manso family to a convent in Puerto Rico. Convento de Porta Coeli, or Basilica Menor de San Juan Bautista y Parroquia Nuestra Señora de los Remedios

BANK OF NEW YORK

Year 1785 (or possibly 1787) - A shipment from Havana arrived in Boston. It was then placed on two stagecoaches to Christoforos Beekman at Hall's Talmadge tavern, 49 Cortland Street, and then on to the Walton Building, Bank of New York. Accompanied by Casimir Theodor Goerck, Isaac Roosevelt and Luis Stone (see chapter 14)

CHAPTER 13

THE PIRATES GRAVEYARD

Anybody who has read Treasure Island or Arthur Ransome's Swallows and Amazons will know that pirate ships ran up black flags sporting the infamous white skull-and-crossbones as they closed in on their prey. The Jolly Roger was first used in monument design in the late-1600s, during the reign of Charles II, as a symbol of mortality. It was seized upon by high seas' pirates, as this was exactly the sentiment they wanted it to convey. As the dreaded pirate ship sailed ever closer to its target, the unfurling of this horrifying promise of their approaching death would have struck terror into the hearts of the simple, highly superstitious seafarers under attack.

Inspecting the tombs of St Andrew's more closely, there is a tombstone leaning against the wall in the corner of the churchyard, under some overhanging trees at the bottom of the footpath steps. Dating to 1684, this one is decorated with an hourglass, just as unsettling in its own way as the skull-and-crossbones. There are two table tombs nearby, one of which belongs to Owen Benfield, and the tomb behind Mr Benfield's, dedicated to Abel Flew, has the skull-and-crossbones design. Dated 'January 1699 in the 49th year of his age'.

St Andrews Church was once occupied by the temple of Venus, which was "beloved by Druids and Phoenicians", and was likely connected to the May Year and the "alignment of the rising sun at Belaine"

The first reference to St. Andrew's Church comes from John Leland in his description of Portland written between 1535 and 1543:

"There is a castelet or pile not far from the streate and is set on a high roche hard by the se cliffes a little above the east end of the Church. The Paroche Chirch taht is but one at this tyme in the isle is large and somewhet low builded in the hanging rootes of an hille by the shore. The Chirch and Paroche is about a mile dem. to go the next way to it from the Kinges New Castelle in the Isle [...] sum say that in tymes past there was a nother Paroche Chirch in the Isle but I there lerned no certente of it. There be very few or utterly no trees in the isle saving the elmes about the Chirch [...] The personage sette in the High Streat is the best building in the Isle. The Bishop of Winchester is the Patrone of the Chirch"

To the south of Church Ope, there was a major landslip on the cliffs in 1734. This is now known as the 'Great Southwell Landslip'; one of the largest ever to occur in the United Kingdom. During this landslip, several hundred metres of cliff slid downwards, in a forward toppling motion, towards the sea. Recovered from this landslip have been an occasional Spanish coin, however it is likely that most finds have gone unreported. Was this the treasure of the Duke of Lerma or other buried treasure?

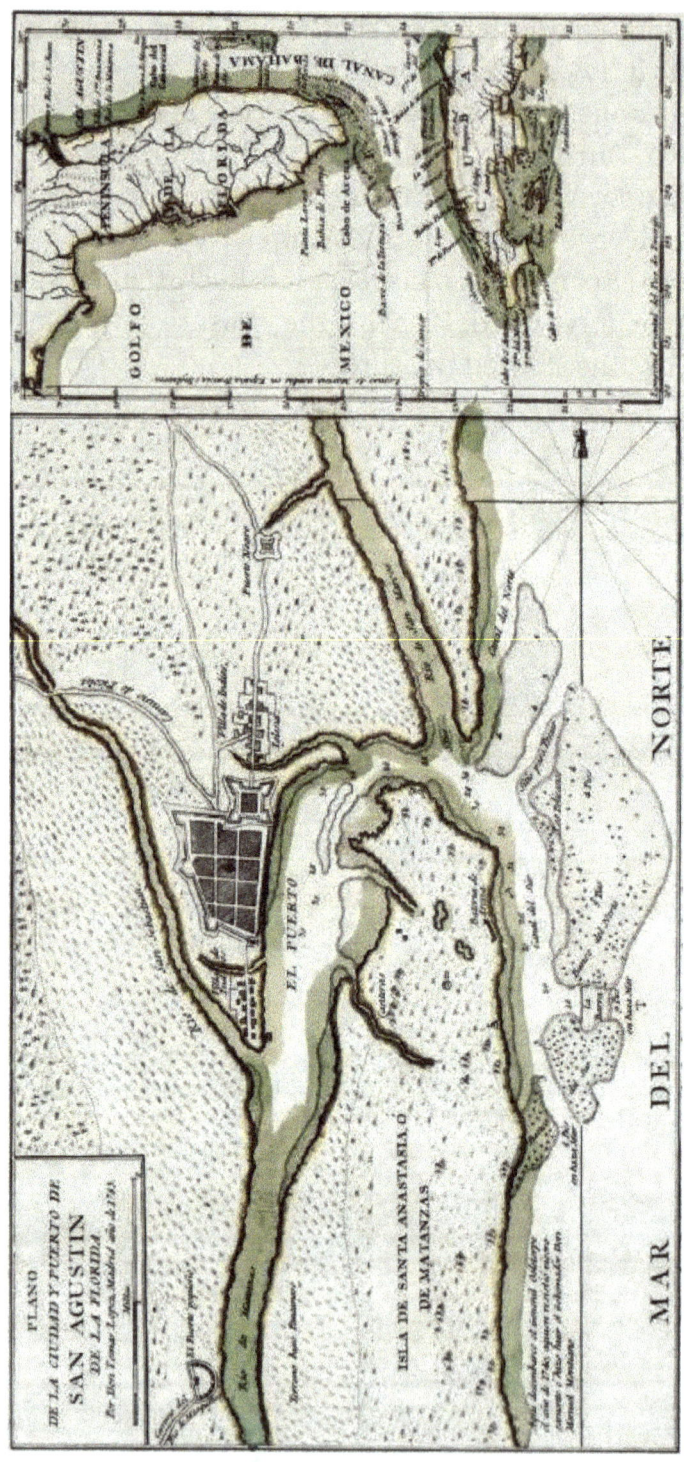

CHAPTER 14

GRACIA REAL DE SANTA TERESA DE MOSE

Between March and November of 1738, Spanish settlers in Florida formed a new town named Gracia Real de Santa Teresa de Mose, two miles to the north of St. Augustine (see map on previous page). Initially, it consisted of 38 men, all fugitive slaves, who had fled to Florida for sanctuary and freedom from enslavement in the Carolinas and Georgia. It came to be known as Fort Mose. By 1759 the village consisted of twenty-two palm thatch huts which housed thirty-seven men, fifteen women, seven boys and eight girls. The people of Mose (pronounced "Moh- say") farmed the land and the men stood guard at the fort or patrolled the frontier. Most of the Carolina fugitives married fellow escapees, Native American, or enslaved people living in St. Augustine.

This town became the first legally sanctioned free black settlement.

Spanish Florida was the African-American slaves' first Promised Land. All of this was prelude to the famous Stono Rebellion in September 1739. Stono was the most violent and the bloodiest uprising of African-American slaves in the 18th century. And it was inspired, in part, by the promise of freedom that awaited escaping slaves in the Spanish haven of

Florida.

Military skirmishes between Spanish and English forces over control of the area between Charleston and St. Augustine began almost as soon as The British established Charleston in 1670, and they escalated dramatically through the eighteenth century. Most of the frontier missions, and St. Augustine itself, were burned down and by the end of first decade of the new century, Spanish activity in East Florida was restricted to St. Augustine.

King Charles II of Spain issued the Edict of 1693 which proclaimed that any African male slave on an English plantation who escaped to Spanish Florida, converted to Catholicism and joined the militia would be rewarded their freedom.

The creation of the first legally sanctioned black settlement wasn't however a smooth path. In 1724, ten runaway slaves reached St. Augustine, assisted by English- speaking Yamassee Indians. Clearly aware of the Spanish King's edict by records of the time that the Spanish king had offered freedom to those seeking baptism and conversion. The royal edict of 1693 was still in force, and Governor Antonio de Benavides initially seems to have honoured it.

In 1729, however, Benavides sold these newcomers at public auction either for his own purse, or to reimburse their owners, fearing the British might act on their threats to recover their losses by force. The most influential citizens of St. Augustine, including the royal accountant, the royal treasurer, military officers, and even some religious officials, acquired valuable new slaves. Others were sold to owners who took them to Havana. In justifying his actions, Benavides explained that these slaves had arrived during a time of peace with England and that he interpreted the 1693 edict to apply only to the original runaways from the British colony. Menendez petitioned the Spanish governor of Florida in which he acted as spokesman for a group of African runaways from Carolina slavery. Menéndez called on the governor to honour Spain's religious sanctuary policy and to free all of the Africans who had come to Florida, only to find themselves re-enslaved. But what transpired was Don Francisco Menéndez Márquez acquired the Mandinga man who would take his name at his Catholic baptism. The African now had a powerful patron — a royal official and a wealthy landowner — Petitioning in support of Menéndez was Chief Jospe, a leader of the Yamasee War with whom Menéndez had fought for several bloody years before they were defeated and fled south.

Menéndez had experienced enslavement by Africans, Englishmen, Yamasees and Spaniards, with only a brief period of freedom during the Yamasee War. Spanish slavery would be different than slavery he had experienced under any others. It is possible that he may have lived some time with the governor himself since his wife took the name Ana María de Escovar.

What is known about Menendez is that he was brought to the Carolinas in the early 18th century from the Mandingo region in Africa, where he may already have been a slave of the Mandinga, who also had a slave culture and considered slaves as property that could be sold, or killed by their masters. The Gambia where he had originated had long been a multi-cultural and multi-lingual world where Mandinga,

Fula, Wolof and Serahuli speakers bartered with Portuguese, Arabic, English, and French so he would possibly have mastered a number of languages.

Raids from Florida by escaped slaves, local Indians and the Spanish triggered an English response in 1728 when Colonel John Palmer led a retaliatory attack against St. Augustine. On that occasion the black militia led by Francisco Menéndez proved one of the city's most effective defence forces. In recognition of that service, the Spanish Crown commended the enslaved forces for their bravery and in 1733 also issued a new decree reiterating its offer of freedom to runaways from Carolina. Francisco Menéndez, however, remained enslaved and so persisted in his efforts to achieve the freedom promised by the Spanish king.

In 1737, with the arrival of a new Spanish governor and the advent of renewed hostilities with the English, his fortunes began to change. Captain Francisco Menéndez solicited freedom for himself and others in a petition that listed thirty-one individuals unjustly enslaved, including some who had been taken to Havana. Governor Montiano granted unconditional freedom to all fugitives from Carolina. The slave owners who had provided loans to the cash-strapped government in return for the slaves vehemently protested their emancipation, but Governor Montiano ruled that the men had ignored the royal determination expressed in repeated decrees and, therefore, all deals were void and all the enslaved would be free He assigned them land two miles north of St. Augustine, whilst recognising Menéndez as leader of the new free black town of Gracia Real de Santa

Teresa de Mose.

In 1740, the English tried to take Spanish Florida and attacked the colony at St. Augustine. The colony's first line of defence was Fort Mose. Led by Captain Francisco Menéndez, the Fort Mose militia briefly lost the Fort to the English but recaptured it and in doing so reputedly metered cruel retribution to the English with all the male soldiers being barbarically castrated.

For a while Menendez sailed with the privateer Captain Pedro de Estrada, with considerable success against British possessions. In 1741, however, Menéndez was captured by the Rhode Island based corsair Revenge, captained by Benjamin Norton, who after interrogation ordered Menendez to have two hundred lashes, which he was lucky to survive, creating a disability that he would carry with him the rest of his days. He was also tied to a canon and threatened with castration in retaliation to what had occurred at Mose.

That August, the Revenge landed at New Providence, in the Bahamas, where its quartermaster vehemently argued before the Vice-Admiralty Court that Menéndez and the other blacks with him should be condemned as slaves and not free men. Menéndez was sold to the lieutenant of the Revenge, William Stone who together formed a lifelong friendship. Stone freed Menendez in 1755 and by 1759 he was again the leader of Mose, albeit short lived.

Fort Mose was abandoned when Florida became part of the British empire after the siege of Havana in 1762. Most of the town's inhabitants, including Captain Menéndez moved to Cuba.

Initially, Captain Francisco Menéndez and eight other free black families were settled at the small fishing village of Regla, across the bay from Havana before being granted new homesteads and relocating to the Matanzas frontier, in the newly created town of San Agustín de la Nueva Florida. The ideal life still was not to be his and the new town failed, with most inhabitants relocating to Havana, Matanzas or Remedios.

Menendez in these last years, although a free man, became dependent in the employ of Manso de Contreras family with his son (or stepson) Jose Escovar Menendez. Jose, who's skin was white, was said to more closely resemble an Englishman than the son of a Mandinga and he would travel under the name of Luis Stone. Luis accompanied a deposit of Manso funds to the bank of New York in 1785.

CHAPTER 15

FORENSIC SCIENCE AND LIDAR MAPPING

Forensic investigation is an evolving and increasingly key tool in modern treasure research. Whilst we use data science to process huge volumes of data related to documented ship, troop and money movements, and scanning centuries of digitised newspapers and records for names, dates and places - looking for patterns we can't see with the naked eye, there are also many documents, letters, manuscripts, charters, and contracts written over time that if we can verify the author, can provide new and exciting lines of enquiry to embarkation and loading at port, shipping routes and who signed for the possession of delivery of shipments.

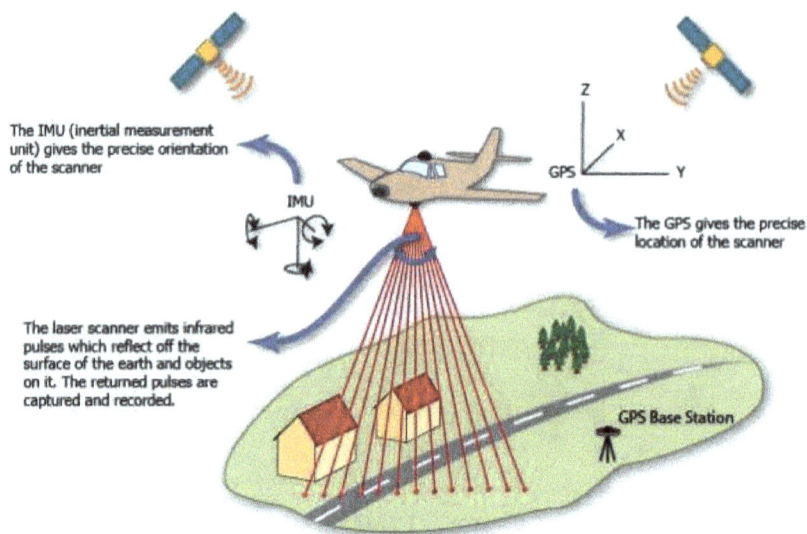

There are different techniques to identify who has handled a specific document or object. Some, such as high definition imagery combined with artificial intelligence, are better suited when non-invasive access is required for delicate or conserved documents, and other techniques such as, fuming, where the underlaying object is less delicate and can provide a base fingerprint for comparison.

From the later thirteenth century onwards, wax seals came to be used by almost all levels of society. The imagery and wording on seals, along with sealing practices and techniques, offer great potential for historical research. Importantly, the back of the wax on which seal impressions are found often retains the image of unique hand prints (finger, thumb or palm)

Impressions of seal matrices in disks of wax, deliberately preserved with their parent documents as part of the legal and administrative process of authentication, survive in great numbers across international archives and private collections.

There has been pioneering work over the last 5 years by a number of commercial and academic organisations. For example, Foster Freeman who are one of the leaders in forensic fingerprint equipment innovation, and the Imprint Seals Project lead by Lincoln and Aberystwyth Universities. We now have the ability to identify and compare fingerprints on seals of key documents from the 17th and 18th centuries.

Utilising high resolution image detection, precise wave bands of illumination from UV improve the fingerprint visualisation and enables us to select the optimum wavelength to generate maximum intensity of fluorescence. Utilising red-light infrared helps us to eliminate background interference. With advances in artificial intelligence we can also digitally enhance the fingerprints. We use a customised camera rig with 20.8 million effective pixels with a 35.9 x 23.9mm CMOS Sensor

Combining a common fingerprinting practice (known as gelatin lifting) with a fuming technique (previously used to reveal finger-marks on fired ammunition) researchers are able to identify fingerprints from objects as well as certain historical documents and letters of key people of interest. It also enables the sequence in which handwriting and finger-marks were added to a document.

Gelatin is placed over a fingerprint that overlaps with some handwriting. The gelatin is then peeled off and placed inside a vacuum-sealed glass box filled with a vapour of a chemical called disulphur dinitride. This vapour binds to the microscopic fingerprint ridges imprinted on the gelatin's surface so that after a few minutes a blue-coloured fingerprint is revealed.

The process tests for a fingerprint that had handwriting written over it and another to test if the handwriting was made on top of the fingerprint. In the former case, the gelatin touches the written ink instead of the fingerprint first so the pattern developed at the end of processing is noticeably different – This enables us to understand which came first, the fingerprint or the handwriting.

Light Detection and Ranging (LiDAR) is an airborne mapping technique, which uses a scanning laser to measure the distance between the aircraft/drone and the ground very accurately. It allows highly detailed representations of relief or terrain models to be generated, often at spatial resolutions of between 25 cm and 2 metres

LiDAR surveys are undertaken during winter months when trees are without leaves, to ensure the most accurate survey of the ground. Up to 500,000 measurements per second are made of the ground, measuring height to an accuracy of better than ±15cm.

LiDAR has been used to detect areas of archaeological significance and uncover the underlying history of a landscape. Researchers have utilized LiDAR to reveal ancient Maya structures, roadways, and other features, as well as generate a three-dimensional picture of a Maya settlement in Belize. LiDAR has also been used to create high-resolution models of Renaissance buildings, such as Florence's Salone dei Cinquecento. It is being utilized in England to find additional sites in the Stonehenge plains.

LiDAR is an important tool looking for evidence of potential locations that might have laid undisturbed for a long time and that are invisible to the eye, but visible with new technology. There are a number of possible locations where part of the

Manso fortune may have been stored, that are currently being investigated, not just through data, but pinpointing potential targets. There are several publicly available blogs of treasure hunters operating around Portland, Taquarey, Yaguajay and Cayo Santa Maria.

CHAPTER 16

WHAT HAPPENED TO CAPTAIN WILLIAM ROBINSON (ROBERTSON)

Captain William Robertson (sometimes spelt Robinson) of the slave ship The London became the captain of the ship called The Hope shortly after the sinking of The London.

The Hope was another slave ship, and it was also owned by the same company that owned The London. Robertson was likely chosen to be the captain of The Hope because of his experience as a sea captain and his knowledge of the slave trade. It is also possible that the owners and backers of the Hope and London were partners with Robertson in some of his exploits, or even the masterminds behind the recovery of the Manso fortune.

The slave ships The London and The Hope were owned by the company called the African Company of Merchants, previously known as the Royal African Company.

The Royal African Company, chartered by the British Crown in 1672, held a monopoly on the slave trade between Africa and the Americas for over 150 years. It is estimated that the company transported over 3 million enslaved people from Africa to the Americas, making it one of the most powerful and influential companies in the British Empire.

The company's ships were well-armed and equipped, allowing them to overpower and capture ships from other countries, further solidifying their dominance in the slave trade. The company also established several forts and trading posts on the African coast, which they used to support their operations and expand their influence.

From 1668 to 1722, the Royal African Company provided gold to the English Mint. Coins made with such gold are designed with an elephant below the bust of the king and/or queen. This gold also gave the coinage its name, the Guinea.

The Royal African Company became the African Company of Merchants in 1752 and played a major role in the transatlantic slave trade, one of the most horrific and inhumane chapters in human history. The company's actions were driven by greed and profit, and they caused immense suffering and loss of life.

The company was abolished in 1807, but the transatlantic slave trade continued for many years after that. It was finally abolished in 1833 after it was found it was still trading slaves illegally, but the legacy of the Royal African Company and the transatlantic slave trade continues to this day.

John Shoolbred is a name that continues to come up in our data science reports in association with Master William Robertson.

Shoolbred (1740-1802) was a Scottish slave trader who was primarily active in London. He was a member of the African Company of Merchants, a British organization established to participate in the transatlantic slave trade. He also served on the company's board of directors.

Shoolbred was a successful slave trader, and he made a great deal of money from his involvement in the trade. However, he was also a controversial figure. In 1777, he was accused of irregularities, including smuggling slaves into British colonies, mistreating enslaved people on his ships, and intercepting funds intended for the American War of Independence for his own benefit. Shoolbred denied the allegations, but they damaged his reputation.

Despite the controversy, Shoolbred remained financially successful until his death in 1802. He was one of the most powerful and influential slave traders in London, and he played a major role in the transatlantic slave trade.

The letters between the two Scots, Shoolbred and Robertson, suggest that they had a relationship of over 20 years during which they planned and successfully undertook highly controversial and violent money-making schemes, such as the transatlantic slave trade.

Robertsons next commission, The Hope, sailed from Liverpool on 15 March 1797 carrying gunpowder and slaves. The ship loaded up with enslaved people and set sail for the Americas. However, The Hope was reported to be caught in a storm and shipwrecked off the coast of Sierra Leone with almost all the enslaved people, who were chained below decks, killed. Robertson was clearly "very lucky" as he was one of the few survivors of the shipwreck.

However, Robertson's luck was starting to run out, as public opinion on the slave trade had started to turn and he was charged with manslaughter. The trial took place in Liverpool, England, in 1797.

Robertson was accused of abandoning ship and leaving the enslaved people on board to die. He was also accused of looting the ship's cargo.

The prosecution presented evidence that Robertson had left the ship before it was fully sunk and that he had taken some of the ship's cargo with him. The defence argued that Robertson had acted in self-defence and that he had taken the cargo to ensure that he had enough supplies to survive.

The jury found Robertson not guilty of manslaughter. However, he was found guilty of looting the ship's cargo and was sentenced to a year in prison at the Liverpool Gaol.

Robertson's acquittal for manslaughter was a controversial decision. Many people believed that he should have been found guilty of his actions, which they felt had led to the deaths of many enslaved people.

The trial of Captain William Robertson highlighted the risks associated with the slave trade. It also showed how difficult it was to hold slave traders accountable for their actions.

According to the Ilfracombe Parish Register, A William Robertson married Jane Smith on February 2, 1801. It was reported that she had previously helped care for his injuries, following the sinking of The London. Was this a seaman who survived the sinking or was this our Captain?

After the shipwreck of The Hope and his year in prison, Captain William Robertson returned to London. There is evidence that he then sailed "accompanied" to Fortaleza, Brazil "with 12 chests" only to immediately return to London where he is now buried in an unmarked grave in Bunhill Fields, a Nonconformist burial ground in the City of London.

Fortaleza – where are these crosses today?

Bunhill Fields was established in 1665 and was used as a burial ground for Nonconformists, or people who did not conform to the Church of England. Many famous people are buried in Bunhill Fields, including Daniel Defoe, John Bunyan, and William Blake.

This story also interlinks with James Ingate who was a successful privateer during the American Revolutionary War. He was known as a quiet and thoughtful man who was not a well-known figure outside of the maritime community. There are no known portraits of him, and no paintings of him in action.

Ingate was born in Dartmouth, England, in 1755. He began his career at sea as a cabin boy, and he eventually rose to the rank of captain. In 1785, he was given command of the brigantine The New Adventure.

The New Adventure was a successful privateer, and it captured over 200 enemy vessels during its career. Ingate was a skilled and daring captain, and he was known for his aggressive tactics. He was also a popular figure among his crew, and he was respected for his fairness and his concern for their welfare.

In 1797 The New Adventure, captained by James Ingate, captured the Spanish ship La Fortuna. Built in Havana, Cuba in 1783, La Fortuna was a 24-gun ship of the line and one of the largest and most powerful ships in the Spanish fleet.

The New Adventure logbook shows that on July 20, 1797, La Fortuna was sailing from Havana to Cadiz in Spain when it was intercepted by the British privateer The New Adventure. As La Fortuna was captured before the outbreak of the French Revolutionary Wars this would make it the first British privateer to capture a Spanish ship of the line in over 100 years.

The New Adventure was a smaller ship than La Fortuna, but it was faster and more manoeuvrable. The New Adventure attacked La Fortuna from the side, and after a brief battle, La Fortuna was forced to surrender.

The capture of La Fortuna was a major victory for the British, and it helped to turn the tide of the war in their favour. The value of the cargo on La Fortuna was estimated to be over £1 million (£192m in today's value). It was a major financial windfall for The New Adventure and its crew, but it was also a major propaganda victory for the British. It showed the world that the British navy was still a powerful force, and it boosted morale among the British people.

Ingate initially retired from the sea after the American Revolutionary War but was persuaded back for future commissions by his friend Master William Robertson. He died in Dartmouth in 1815.

CHAPTER 17

THE OTHER MANSO LINEAGE

(oidor) Manso de Contreras grew up on the Island of Margarita, off the coast of Venezuala, where his father was Governor. His mother Eugenia Simon, a native of Becerril was also known as Quirós de Bardecí. She was the aunt of Francisco Negrete, alderman and attorney general of Puerto Rico.

Assisting his father, he held a number of different positions in the local government such as Regidor and Alcalde Ordinario, becoming the islands representative in Spain. Later he was appointed Governor of Santa Marta and Riohacha travelling there in 1592 with his close servant and friend Juan de Tudela.

As a reward for his defence of this post he was promoted to Fiscal of the Audiencia of Santo Domingo, replacing Buenaventura Cuadrado in April 1602, with a rank of Oidor granted in May 1603. He had strong family ties in Margarita where his wife resided, Puerto Rico where his father was born, and Santo Domingo where he was related to the influential Bardeci family.

In 1605 he accepted a commission from the Governor, Osorio, to go to Cuba to bring back residents of La Yaguana who had run away to Bayamo after resisting a forced relocation and interference in some smuggling activities. Travelling via Cartagena where he attended to some personal business for more than a month, he arrived in Cuba, put his main commission to one side, and headed into the centre looking for smugglers whilst having had some time in Havana suffering from gout.

Governor Osario was unimpressed and made separate arrangements to recover the population of La Yaguana, so when Manso finally arrived in Bayamo he could not find them. Osario began collecting testimonies on what he saw as unacceptable behaviour from Manso, which included accepting bribes, abusing his power and abusing women.

By 1608, when Manso returned, his influence was clearly damaged. Complaining to the King he eventually arranged a transfer as Audiencia of Panama arriving in 1609 and serving for 10 years. His final post was as alcalde de crimen in Mexico, but he didn't last the year before he died.

CHAPTER 18

TIMELINE

1598: King Philip of Spain sent his cousin, Francisco Manso de Contreras – to the Caribbean to seek and destroy French and Dutch pirates and seize their stolen treasure, whilst earning a percentage.

1603: Francisco ventured into Cuba and became enchanted with the island. Sending for his brother, Antonio in 1606, with their wives they settled in the colonial town of Remedios near the northern coast. Over the next 100 years they became exceedingly rich.

1701: Bartolome, son of Andres, the grandson of Antonio, marries Isabel Hernandez de Medina y Vidal and inherits the majority of the Manso fortune. The largest portion of the Manso fortune that was held in chests (as opposed to property or slaves) was moved to Yaguajay when Bartolome purchased, for $4,500, the hacienda in July 1697 from GONZALEZ DE LA CRUZ Y CRESPO (Jose), a priest who was a close family friend and who had baptised Isabel Hernandez de Medina y Vida in 1671.

1704: Becoming increasingly alarmed by world events it was decided that some of the fortune would be transported to Santa Rosa de la Eminencia, Margarita, where family descending from Francisca, daughter of Francisco, who had emigrated to Isle Magarita in 1585 and where several members of the Manso family had held positions of authority, including Margarita's representation in Spain. There was also a possible transport to London at this time.

1710: Report of a heavy transport of seven chests from the Manso family to a convent in Puerto Rico. Convento de Porta Coeli, or, Basilica Menor de San Juan Bautista y Parroquia Nuestra Señora de los Remedios

1762 August: 8th August - British capture Havana as part of the 7 year war with France, when Spain decides to intervene on the side of France the British took the Spanish completely unawares.

1762 September: 6th September - Transport ships carrying part of the Manso fortune, escorted by Royal Highlanders Regiment, briefly dock in New York before continuing towards Halifax. 10th September - two transports dock in Bridgewater. 12 September - two transports escorted by His Majesty's Ship, Aldborough to Plymouth.

1762 October: 13 October - Manso chests signed for in Plymouth by Francis Baring. 29 October - Sloop "The Falmouth" arrives Oak Island. With the help of William Nurenburg, a talented mining engineer, the chests are buried at the Money Pit.

1762 December: 25th December – the bank that will become the UK's most prestigious merchant bank is formed. Barings Bank.

1771: Aborted recovery of the Oak Island deposit following suspected plague on board from Russian sailors from St Petersburg.

1776: US Declaration of Independence. Large deposit of gold and jewels sent to London on the ship El Titan. Escorted by Jose Manso de Contreras y Perez del Prado, who went under the name of Jeronimo Paez de Villa Franca. When Bartolome the younger married Josefina de Loyola y Monteagudo, they had four children. The heir, Luis, who under Spanish Law should have inherited - died in infancy, and the three girls, María Isabel del Santísimo Sacramento, María Dolores de la Resurrección and María Manuela de San Agustín, were cloistered nuns in the convent of Santa Clara in the City of Havana where their family friend and priest Gonzales de La Cruz y Crespo was buried. They tool with them a small part of the family fortune that would be shipped to London on the El Titan.

1784: Rumour of another large deposit being sent to London (Barings) or to The Bank of New York. This is being investigated.

1789: French Revolution. Increasing tension in Cuba following revolution with threat of insurrection, and high-profile leaders such as Nicolás Morales. Risk that a possible revolution could lead to fortune being confiscated. A further deposit is sent to London.

1793: France declares war on Britain once more. Britain saw the French Colonies in the West Indies as an opportunity. British early gains damaged by yellow fever amongst troops.

1795: British General Abercromby and Rear Admiral Christian make considerable success taking Dutch and French colonies. Soon St Lucia, St Vincent and Grenada were in British hands.

1796 June: French prisoners of war are loaded onto transport ships heading for UK prisons. Convoy lead by HMS Gangees starts to assemble in Basseterre Bay, St Kitts. Four transports leave early with the intention of the recovery of the Manso fortune from Oak Island. They recover the fortune and re-join the convoy 100 miles off Newfoundland in September.

1796 November: The four transports carrying the Manso fortune slip away from The Gangees convoy and head for Ilfracombe on North Devon Coast. The New adventure arrives and unloads safely, The London is scuttled outside the harbour when the fortune has been safely unloaded.

1796 December: The surviving French prisoners of war transported to Stapleton prison, Bristol. Col Commandant Heaurmaux of Fort Charlotte, St Vincent and his wife are released into parole in Chippenham. Transport of recovered "chests & trunks" from Ilfracomebe via Chambercombe Manor to the Square & Compass a Public House with strong links to the freemasons in Launceston, Cornwall

1803: Barings Bank provided finance to the United States government for the purchase of Louisiana from Napoleon Bonaparte in 1803. This doubled the size of The United States. $3 million down payment in gold, the remainder of the purchase was made in United States bonds. James Monroe negotiated the purchase. He was also a customer and advisor to Barings.

1808: Investigating a large transport of "supplies" to the remote town of Taquari(Taquarey) what is now within state of Rio Grande do Sul, Brazil. Transport arranged by Snr H Akwa,(Aqua) a colonist originally from Neu-Kolonie in Russia, a new town of Wolgadeutsche (Volga Germans). (Map of Taquari on following page.)

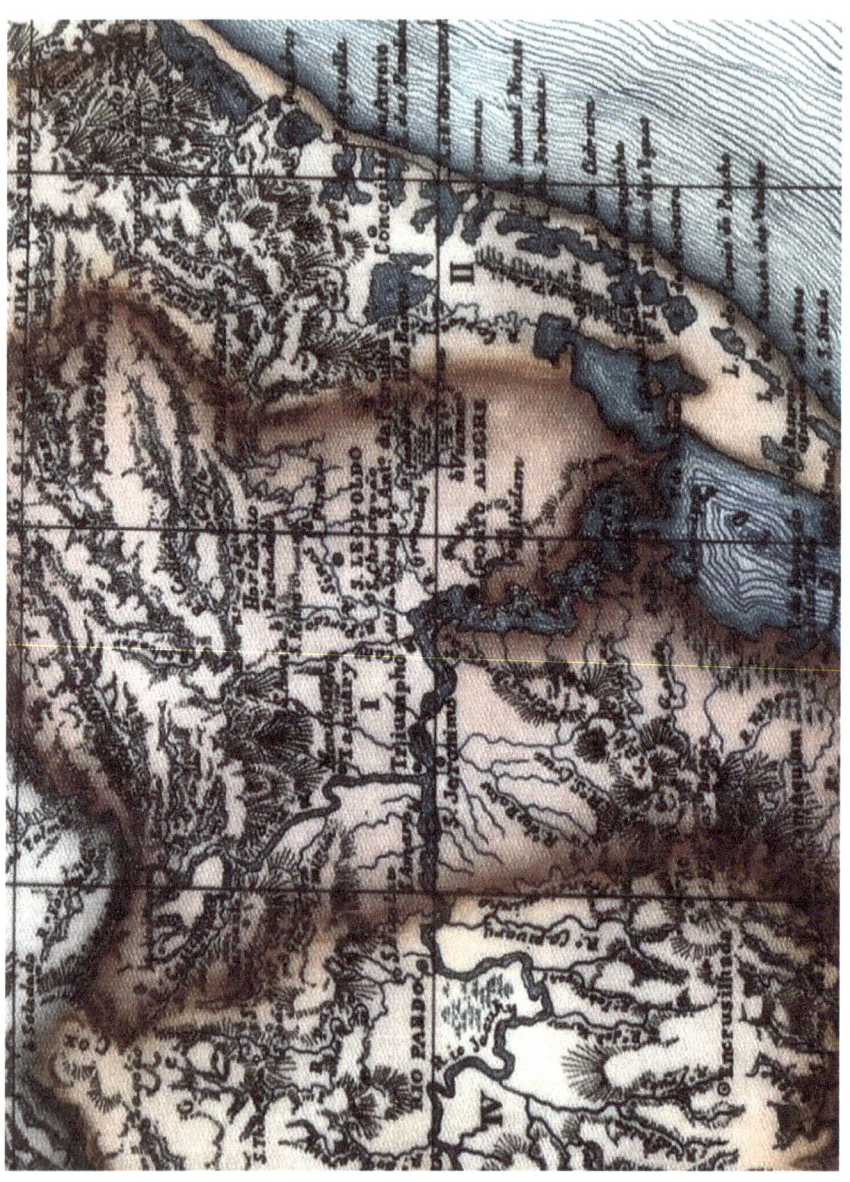

CHAPTER 19

BARINGS BANK

Just off the lobby, at Dutch bank ING's London office on Moorgate, is an unremarkable door. It is easy to miss; it looks identical to the surrounding wall panels, other than its handle. Behind it is another door, with a sign warning that the room ahead has a reduced oxygen supply, and that visitors must leave immediately if an alarm sounds. Inside lies the legacy of one of the world's oldest merchant banks.

The clandestine Bearing Archive, a collection of centuries-old documents and materials charts the story of the bank that started life the same year that the transports arrived from Cuba.

The room has its oxygen and humidity controlled so that if a fire broke out it could not spread, and staff are told not to spend more than a few hours inside without taking a thirty-minute break.

Although economic historians, and other researchers travel from around the world to work in the nearby reading room – where notes must be taken in pencil because of the risk of ink getting on documents – the archive has remained largely hidden.

Barings had an illustrious client list, including The Russian Royal Family, Bonaparte's nephew, Napoleon III, as well as US Presidents, James Monroe and Franklin Roosevelt. By 1818, Bearings was called, "the sixth great European power", after Great Britain, France, Prussia, Austria and Russia.

CHAPTER 20

FAMILIA MANSO

In 2021, excited rumours swirled around Cuba that the Cuban leader Fidel Castro was close to repatriating the Manso fortune. Hundreds of people from all over Cuba, the Caribbean, and as far away as Oregon, California, and the Philippines queued to obtain copies of birth certificates that might prove their claim to the inheritance. They claimed that President Castro was secretly negotiating with the British government and that the return of the fortune was imminent.

Some believe that Cuba already had some funds in its banks and was awaiting additional bank transfers from England. According to the rumours, the Cuban government would not distribute the money in lump sums. Instead, recipients would receive a few thousand dollars upfront and $350 per month for the rest of their lives.

Alas the inheritors are still waiting and accuse the British and Cuban governments, as well as the Vatican, of ongoing secret negotiations.

One group of heirs, based in Miami, has recently attempted to purchase million-dollar properties in South Florida using typewritten documents from the church archives in Remedios as proof of their ancestry as collateral. It is unclear whether the heirs were successful in their attempts to purchase the properties, but I guess not!

In Cuba, regional Manso de Contreras committees have been established for several years. These committees meet regularly, with government permission, to discuss the progress of the investigations and plans for the distribution of the money, should it ever be recovered.

In Miami, some of the descendants have a website and have secured legal counsel from one of the most prestigious law firms in the country. Through their relatives in Cuba, the Miami heirs have managed to obtain old wills and classified documents from the Cuban government that they claim prove the existence of the fortune. The Miami Cubans say they are prepared to sue the Cuban government if officials decide to exclude them from their inheritance.

In Cuba, the committees have reportedly pledged 25% of their shares of the inheritance to the Cuban government in exchange for the government's cooperation, although in fairness most are realistic enough to assume the shoe is on the other foot.

In response to multiple approaches by individuals and lawyers, who present evidence of relatives who may have deposited money at the Bank of England or one of it's forebears, the answer from their spokeswomen is always the same "We have absolutely no knowledge of the deposits, only the rumours," spokesmen say. That does not impress Cubans, who at times have protested outside the British Consulate in Miami, accusing the Queen of robbing them. Ten demonstrators were arrested in the past.

In the 1940s, a glimmer of hope emerged for ordinary Cubans who believed they were heirs to the lost Manso de Contreras fortune. Sensational newspaper articles claimed that the Bank of England could no longer afford the interest payments on the fortune, and urged all heirs in Cuba to come forward and claim their inheritance. This sparked a mad rush to Remedios, the town where the Manso de Contreras family had once resided, to obtain the necessary documents. But no money was recovered and there is no evidence of The Bank of England had advertised for heirs at all.

The full story of the Manso de Contreras fortune was told in a series of highly sensationalist articles published in the Cuban magazine Bohemia in 1946. These articles were photocopied and passed from hand to hand in villages all across the country, igniting the dreams of many who believed they were entitled to a share of the fortune.

In 1947, one of the family members hired a lawyer to retrace the steps of Joseph Manso de Contreras in London. But just as the lawyer was about to complete his research, he disappeared, never to be found. Local rumours swirled about who was to blame, with some pointing the finger at the Vatican, the Cuban secret police and more conspiracies within the London financial institutions. The disappearance was treated seriously enough for the British Police to investigate.

Even whilst researching this book the Manso fortune was again back in the news. This time with Pope Francis, in his first full week back at the Vatican in 2023 following abdominal surgery, he met with Cuba's president, and speculation was rife that once more the Cuban government was trying to repatriate the funds back to Cuba, this time from the Vatican Bank. The Holy See's brief statement of the private meeting with President Miguel Diaz-Canel gave no details of what the pontiff and the Cuban leader discussed, and when asked by journalists if the conversation included the lost fortune of Manso de Contreras, the official response was "no comment". There have been strong rumours that the Vatican are one of the key shareholders of the Manso Tontine, following Ernesto Pacelli being present at the tontine re-issue meeting in 1882 at Bradgate Park representing Vincento Gioacchino Raffaele Luigi Pecci, Pope Leo XIII. There is however no modern data trail to substantiate that.

CHAPTER 21

THE OAK ISLAND CODE - CONCLUSION

The data that underpins this research has shown how the Manso family had amassed a huge fortune, possibly one of the largest private fortunes in the world at that time. The value of that fortune, over 227 years, at a modest interest rate of 5% per year, could top £1.16 sextillion today. I didn't know sextillion was a number either!

So we get to the final question. Where is the lost fortune of Manso de Contreras?

The bad news is that the story that winds through the data of time doesn't place it in the Money Pit at Oak Island, or at least not anymore. A small part indeed was once there until it was removed and smuggled to England in 1796, where at least one part of that was on the ship, The London, that was scuttled at Ilfracombe on the 10th of October.

But if you thought you had a claim to that fortune, reading the data, where would you plant your spade?

I would advise you to put your spade away and start looking through the data, and specifically for who holds shares in the Manso Tontine. It was initially created by William Paterson on behalf of the Manso family, and by 1882, this rolling tontine was being administered by Sir Frederick Johnstone, 8th Baronet of Westerhall. It was reissued in 1952 and almost certainly again in 2023 following the death of Queen Elizabeth II in 2022.

There is one final clue, a postcard, a picture of the front of which appears in one of the shortest chapters in this book (Chapter 11), held in the historical archives of a London bank. Which bank? I cannot tell you, as they would not allow me to share that information. However, if you have read this book, you may have a couple of ideas.

The postcard is in the name of Mary Buckingham, and it is clear that she was a shareholder of the Manso Tontine and that this was her way of confirming that she was still alive after the death of another shareholder. Whether she was really still alive or not seems to be part of the problem as there was suspicion, she had previously died and a speculative relative didn't want to lose their share of the tontine by claiming she had got better. Indeed many suspected miraculous resurrections appear to be related to tontines. Today, modern-world confirmation is by biometric recognition and blockchain rather than a letter or postcard, but this is actually good news, especially for data scientists, as data, as we have explained, always, always leaves a trail!

The surviving relatives of Manso Contreras have not given up hope that one day they will receive a share of that wealth their ancestors had acquired. They have made representations to UK and US Governments, The Bank of England, hired lawyers and private investigators, protested outside embassies and even had conversations with more than one Pope!

I would like to think those people in Cuba, who are generally not wealthy individuals, could one day, very soon, share a part of the worlds largest lost fortune.

¡Que Dios te acompañe!

ABOUT THE AUTHOR

David is passionate about using technology to make a positive impact on the world. As a technology innovator with a long career in developing new technologies to solve complex problems, he is now using his expertise in data science and artificial intelligence to find hidden treasures around the world. He believes treasure hunting can be more than just an adventure; it can also be a way to learn about history, culture, and the environment.

www.ingramcontent.com/pod-product-compliance
Lightning Source LLC
Chambersburg PA
CBHW052059110526
44591CB00013B/2278